Active Literacy Across the Curriculum

T0244335

Help students become more confident and successful readers, writers, and thinkers in today's world. In this new edition of a bestseller, highly acclaimed author and speaker Heidi Hayes Jacobs offers practical ideas for closing the literacy gap by teaching classic literacies (reading, writing, speaking, and listening) along with essential new literacies (digital, media, and global). This expanded second edition features Heidi's latest work on the new literacies and provides enhanced versions of strategies designed to help educators integrate critical language skills into their daily operational curriculum. These strategies include:

- Revising and expanding the role of all teachers so that they see themselves as classical language and contemporary literacy teachers;
- Separating vocabulary into three distinctive types with distinctive instructional approaches to sustain and extend independent language development;
- Building creative and visual notetaking and sketchnoting strategies;
- Designing media projects for every class level and employing a consistent editing and revision policy for writing assignments;
- Using a formal approach to develop speaking skills through four discussion types to increase civil public discourse;
- Employing direct technical instruction that promotes the use of the human voice and body as a speaking and communication instrument;
- Using Curriculum Mapping to develop formal benchmark assessments for active literacy and new literacy cultivation in every subject and on every level.

Each chapter is focused on a specific strategy and includes practical examples so you can easily implement the ideas, no matter what grade level or subject area you teach.

Dr. Heidi Hayes Jacobs is President of Curriculum Designers, Inc. She is a bestselling author and an internationally recognized expert in the fields of curriculum and instruction, having consulted on issues pertaining to Curriculum Mapping, dynamic instruction, and 21st-century strategic planning.

Other Eye on Education
Titles Available from Routledge
(www.routledge.com/eyeoneducation)

From Texting to Teaching:
Grammar Instruction in a Digital Age
Jeremy Hyler and Troy Hicks

Create, Compose, Connect!
Reading, Writing, and Learning with Digital Tools
Jeremy Hyler and Troy Hicks

Close Reading the Media:
Literacy Lessons and Activities for Every Month
of the School Year
Frank Baker

Write, Think, Learn:
Tapping the Power of Daily Student Writing
Across the Content Areas
Mary K. Tedrow

Writing Behind Every Door:
Teaching Common Core Writing in the Content Areas
Heather Wolpert-Gawron

The Literacy Coaching Handbook:
Working with Teachers to Improve Student Achievement
Diana Sisson and Betsy Sisson

The Multimedia Writing Toolkit:
Helping Students Incorporate Graphics and Videos for
Authentic Purposes, Grades 3–8
Sean Ruday

Your First Year:
How to Survive and Thrive as a New Teacher
Todd Whitaker, Madeline Whitaker, and Katherine Whitaker

Intentional Innovation:
How to Guide Risk-Taking, Build Creative Capacity, and
Lead Change
AJ Juliani

Active Literacy Across the Curriculum

Connecting Print Literacy with Digital, Media, and Global Competence, K–12

Second Edition

Heidi Hayes Jacobs

Routledge
Taylor & Francis Group

NEW YORK AND LONDON

Second edition published 2018
by Routledge
711 Third Avenue, New York, NY 10017

and by Routledge
2 Park Square, Milton Park, Abingdon, Oxon, OX14 4RN

Routledge is an imprint of the Taylor & Francis Group, an informa business

© 2018 Taylor & Francis

The right of Heidi Hayes Jacobs to be identified as author of
this work has been asserted by her in accordance with sections
77 and 78 of the Copyright, Designs and Patents Act 1988.

All rights reserved. No part of this book may be reprinted
or reproduced or utilised in any form or by any electronic,
mechanical, or other means, now known or hereafter invented,
including photocopying and recording, or in any information
storage or retrieval system, without permission in writing from
the publishers.

Trademark notice: Product or corporate names may be
trademarks or registered trademarks, and are used only for
identification and explanation without intent to infringe.

First edition published by Eye On Education 2006

Library of Congress Cataloging-in-Publication Data
Names: Jacobs, Heidi Hayes, author.
Title: Active literacy across the curriculum : connecting print
   literacy with digital, media, and global competence, K-12 /
   by Heidi Hayes-Jacobs.
Description: Second edition. | New York : Routledge, 2017. |
   "First edition published by Eye On Education 2006"—
   T.p. verso. | Includes bibliographical references.
Identifiers: LCCN 2017024173 (print) | LCCN 2017034314 (ebook) |
   ISBN 9781315693927 (ebook) | ISBN 9781138909571 (paperback)
Subjects: LCSH: Language arts—Correlation with content subjects. |
   Language experience approach in education. | Direct instruction.
Classification: LCC LB1576 (ebook) |
   LCC LB1576 .J256 2017 (print) | DDC 372.6—dc23
LC record available at https://lccn.loc.gov/2017024173

ISBN: 978-1-138-50299-4 (hbk)
ISBN: 978-1-138-90957-1 (pbk)
ISBN: 978-1-315-69392-7 (ebk)

Typeset in Palatino
by Apex CoVantage, LLC

Chapter opener art © **Silvia Rosenthal Tolisano**

Printed and bound in the United States of America by Sheridan

Contents

Foreword

While I admire all the creative and contemporary ways Heidi Hayes Jacobs improves our educational landscape with her bold ideas, this particular book and its overall message are near and dear. The first edition of *Active Literacy Across the Curriculum* is the first book I ever read by Heidi, back before I had the good fortune of knowing her personally. The ideas resonated with me immediately as a teacher who taught both language arts and science. I eagerly sought out professional texts, of which there were few, that would help me develop my expertise with content-area literacy. This book offered multiple strategies to improve my professional practice and the learning of my students. In particular, I was forever changed by the idea of "mental velcro": how we get the learning to stick. I continue to look at my professional work through this mental velcro lens, even now.

These many years later, and I know Heidi to be a connector, a bridge. She connects people and ideas. She connects analysis to big, bold actions. She connects the contemporary and the classical. She connects the timely and the timeless. She is a living example of one of the key ideas from this second edition of *Active Literacy Across the Curriculum*: Contemporary literacy is built around the ways we connect to each other, not just the ways we communicate. Before the 21st century and our myriad ways to connect, literacy was mostly about communication: reading the evening paper, listening to the radio, writing telegrams. But now that we have changed our audiences from local to global, communication is just a slice of the literate pie. In order to savor the whole pie, purposeful and relevant connections around convergent multimedia are crucial for the totality of what being literate in the 21st century means.

In the decade since *Active Literacy Across the Curriculum* was first published, the strategies we previously employed to teach students how to be better readers, writers, and speakers has shifted dramatically. What it means to be literate has shifted dramatically. The way that people access and acquire knowledge has been revolutionized. The fact that the book you have in your hand could be read as a traditional print text, accessed in an app on your tablet or computer, or read on your phone is indicative of the explosion of the myriad ways we now interact and connect with reading, writing, speaking, and listening. The landscape of opportunities, combined with a plethora of new ways to interact and instruct, requires a new emphasis on literacies that go well beyond traditional print. All types of media live everywhere, all the time now. This round-the-clock access to information and media is changing the way we communicate, learn, and live.

And connect.

For our students, who have grown up in this "everything, all the time" environment, this roaring din is near constant in their daily lives, whereas it is mostly foreign to adults who remember the good old days of dusty newspapers and three TV channels. That said, constant access doesn't necessarily mean that quality learning is happening or that messages aren't getting diluted in their translations. In fact, constant access without thoughtful filtering, explanation, discussion, and relevance is detrimental to critical analysis and the learning process. Likewise, superficial connections do not engender deep thinking, evaluation, or purposeful choices beyond which emoji students might choose to visualize their text messages.

We need students to be mindful in ways they've never had the opportunity to be before now. In this second edition of *Active Literacy Across the Curriculum*, Heidi explores that mindfulness as she connects traditional print literacy to new literacies that impact learning in this age of convergence and perpetual media flow. Heidi writes that she "sees these literacies as mutually dependent, rather than classical literacies being at odds with the new." I agree. We want students to be classically literate in reading, writing, speaking, and listening, but also literate in filtering, connecting, curating, choosing, commenting, tweeting, notetaking, creating, and more when they engage digital, media, and global literacies.

To accomplish this contemporary goal of embracing new literacies and strategically shifting instructional practices around what educators should cut, keep, or create, Heidi offers enhanced versions of literacy strategies new to this second edition:

STRATEGY ONE: Revise the role of all teachers to see themselves as contemporary literacy educators and enhance opportunities for students to interact with classical and contemporary literacies everywhere with every teacher.

STRATEGY TWO: Classify three distinct types of vocabulary that have different instructional approaches, including the integrated use of digital tools across all classrooms, K–12. This is especially important as students move into the upper elementary and on into secondary school where assumptions about a student's vocabulary could be detrimental to continued learning.

STRATEGY THREE: Expand the notion of notetaking to something more creative, visual, and interactive, such as sketchnoting, which promotes interactive analysis and extraction of relevant details, rather than what Heidi describes as "a passive-receptive approach." Sketchnoting, too, as a contemporary replacement to more traditional forms of notetaking, is inclusive of Heidi's four different notetaking forms.

STRATEGY FOUR: Create a consistent editing and revision policy around media projects, publications, and productions, including those engaged with digital tools, for every learner in every content area and grade level.

STRATEGY FIVE: Increase public discourse and speaking skills through four discussion types employing modern media for feedback, analysis, and argument. Additionally, these discussion types can be engaged in the physical classroom or across virtual learning platforms with an emphasis on sharpening critical and creative thinking.

STRATEGY SIX: Support direct instruction for building confident and poised speakers using video and audio tools for growth and feedback.

STRATEGY SEVEN: Document classical and contemporary literacies in every subject and grade level through the Curriculum Mapping process. This creates opportunities for agreed-upon literacy strategies and practices, as well as opportunities for continued contemporary upgrades across all grade levels and content areas when the maps are reviewed.

Through these seven strategies Heidi makes the case that active literacy is a shared responsibility amongst all stakeholders in a school system and that the many facets which comprise contemporary literacy are essential learning for every student's learning journey. Students need continual and consistent practice with these literacies in every class and grade level so that they can communicate and connect with anyone, regardless of geographic location.

In this second edition of *Active Literacy Across the Curriculum*, Heidi connects refreshed contemporary literacy strategies to contemporary teachers in every class and in every grade level. She connects teachers to digital tools to interact, to connect globally, and to make media. She connects ideas about different types of vocabulary, different forms of notetaking, and different types of discussion. She invites teachers to connect their work to each other by documenting their contemporary upgrades in a collaborative curriculum map. This culture of connection increases transparency and opportunities to collaborate as literate 21st-century citizens.

This is how we prepare our learners for the future.

Michael Fisher
Digigogy.com
@fisher1000
Amherst, NY
March, 2017

Acknowledgments

Teachers led me to engage in writing *Active Literacy*. I have many vivid memories of groups of staff members discussing and crafting ways to shape curriculum and instruction that would reel in their students into loving reading, writing, speaking, and listening. They are fierce advocates for their learners and inspire thought and action. But it is the sense of frustration in returning back to the isolation of a classroom after those discussions that got to me. These teachers want to collaborate on literacy support for learners together and consistently. I thank them for their inspiration. The creative and spirited images created by Silvia Tolisano that open each chapter are a testament to her astonishing abilities. She read with understanding, rendering the gist of each chapter into a sketchnote. Silvia has stretched my thinking for years, and I marvel at her abilities. I extend my warmest regards and deepest thanks to the brilliant Amy Benjamin from upstate New York who actually makes grammar fascinating. Mike Fisher's personal and generous foreword moves me, given his creativity and prominence in the field of digital learning.

One of the most talented literacy specialists in the country, Jeanne Tribuzzi, has a grasp on how to bring a passion for reading into every classroom. She has been a valued colleague, providing feedback and suggestions for professional development for years. I am dazzled by the power and depth of the work at Teachers College Reading and Writing Project under the direction of the brilliant Lucy Calkins, whom I have known for many, many years. As a curriculum designer, it has been a gift for me to periodically interact with her faculty at TC and learn from their approach. My colleague, Marie Alcock, has provided consistently valuable feedback for the past twenty years that informs my practice and imagination. She is a remarkable educator and human being. Special thanks to the patient

Lauren Davis from Routledge, who is a supportive and insightful editor. In the field of literacy, the initial books of Dr. Rachel Billmeyer first opened my eyes to the possibilities of connecting learner-friendly language strategies into teacher-friendly instruction. Family is core to all learning, and I am deeply grateful for mine. Each one is remarkable: Jeffrey, Rebecca, Matt, Gideon, and Naomi. Thank you.

Meet the Author

Dr. Heidi Hayes Jacobs, creator of Curriculum21, is also the founder and president of Curriculum Designers, Inc. Heidi has served as an education consultant to thousands of schools nationally and internationally. She works with schools and districts K–12 on issues and practices pertaining to creating a 21st-century learning environment, upgrading Curriculum Mapping, and strategic planning. Her numerous articles have appeared in professional journals. Heidi is the author of twelve books, the most recent being *Bold Moves for Schools: How We Create Remarkable Learning Environments*, co-authored with Marie Alock and published by ASCD. Her other books include *The Curriculum Mapping Planner: Templates and Tools for Effective Professional Development*, co-authored with Ann Johnson, and *Curriculum 21: Essential Education for A Changing World*, which was selected as the worldwide member book by ASCD. She created the first LumiBook with SINET titled *Mapping to the Core: Integrating the CCSS into Your Local School Curriculum* in 2012. Heidi's book series, *Contemporary Perspectives on the New Literacies* includes *Mastering Digital Literacy, Mastering Media Literacy, Mastering Global Literacy*, and *Leading the New Literacies* (Solution Tree, 2014–2015).

Working with a range of organizations, Jacobs has online courses with PBS Teacherline and PD360 and has consulted to groups ranging from state education departments, ECIS, the Near East School Association, the College Board, the Kennedy Center, the Peace Corps World Wise Schools, Carnegie Hall, the Tri-Association of Central America, Mexico, and the Caribbean, the United Nations Council on Teaching about the UN, the International Baccalaureate, the NY State Higher Education Commission, and the CCSSO workgroup on Global Competencies. In 2014 Heidi received the MAIS International Educator Award in Seville, Spain, for contributions to global education.

Introduction

Essential Strategies to Nurture the Literate Learner:
Classical and Contemporary

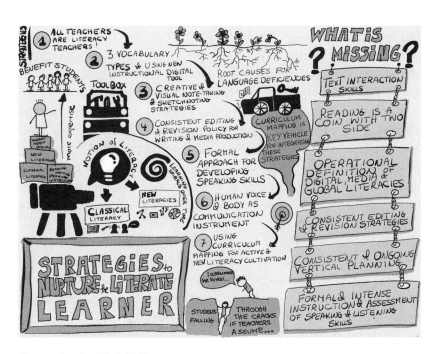

Illustration by Silvia Tolisano

A new edition of a book suggests a refreshed and updated revision. Given the learning revolution that has emerged over the past decade with the infusion of new technologies, any book on supporting literacy development must reflect that impact. The aim here is straightforward: to provide a set of cross-curricular literacy strategies that address problems directly affecting student performance and engagement in the 21st century. Key is that the "notion" of literacies will be explored and considered both in terms of classical literacy (reading, writing, speaking, and listening) and new literacies (digital, media, and global). The recommended strategies have the potential for assisting learners, especially if a faculty makes a school-wide commitment to employ them. This is not to say that all teachers will instruct their students in the same way. The point is that the vast inconsistencies in language usage expectations and the integration of new literacies among teachers are contributing factors to the vast inconsistencies in student performance. The implication is clear: when teachers raise their professional expertise with both classical and new literacies, their students are the direct beneficiaries.

The focus in this book is through the lens of curriculum design and articulation for grades K–12 and is addressed to classroom teachers. My contention is that there is a need for fundamental revision. Many of our current practices inhibit the effectiveness of teachers and produce some of the factors leading to academic illiteracy. These need to be replaced with more effective approaches. This book does not purport to be a resource guide for reading specialists. It attempts to give classroom teachers, many of whom have not had the benefit of special reading training, a set of tools for integrating critical language skills coupled with digital, media, and global literacy capacities into their daily operational curriculum. The needed skills are laid out in a planning model to be implemented in a school or district under the assumption that learning is cumulative and that skills spiral over time. Curriculum Mapping (Jacobs, 1997, 2004, 2012) as a critical school-wide and district-wide tool for implementing and monitoring these strategies is described at the end of the book as a vehicle for formally integrating and monitoring student progress in the demonstration of these strategies in their products and performances. The strategies are as follows:

1. Revising and expanding the role of all teachers (all subjects and levels) so that they see themselves as classical language and contemporary literacy teachers.
2. Separating vocabulary into three distinctive types with distinctive instructional approaches employing new digital tools to sustain and extend independent language development in every classroom K–12.
3. Building creative and visual notetaking and sketchnoting strategies for extraction and reaction, as opposed to a passive-receptive approach.
4. Designating and employing a consistent editing and revision policy for writing and developing media projects for every class on a developmental level K–12 to media publications and productions for each learner.
5. Using a formal approach to develop speaking skills through four discussion types to increase civil public discourse employing modern media for feedback and review.
6. Employing direct technical instruction that promotes the use of the human voice and body as a speaking and communication instrument to develop poise, confidence, and power for each student in every classroom using video and audio tools to support growth and feedback.
7. Using Curriculum Mapping as a unifying school-wide vehicle to develop formal benchmark assessments for active literacy and new literacy cultivation in every subject and on every level.

These seven strategies can be woven into each classroom through the use of Curriculum Mapping, which provides a technological means of communicating and designing instructional solutions. Curriculum Mapping is in itself a strategy for implementing the other six strategies and is described in the last chapter of this book.

In order to contextualize the strategies, let us consider some of the intrinsic causes that have created the literacy gaps in our curriculum. These gaps help to explain why students in the United States are not performing at levels worthy of their ability and, subsequently, why they do not meet standards. Consider the findings in the *Progress for International Student Assessment* report every three years. The United States ranked 22nd for the ability of fifteen-year-old students on reading literacy and 40th for mathematical literacy of fifteen-year-old students (National Center for Educational Statistics, 2015). I believe a key reason for this disappointing performance is that too many American students have weak reading, writing, speaking, and listening skills in all of their subjects. The following are some fundamental root causes for these language deficiencies.

What Is Missing?

Missing: Text Interaction Skills
Consider the following:

> You are sitting in an airport terminal waiting for your plane and reading a magazine article. You look up at the monitor to check flight departure times. Suddenly you realize that you don't remember a thing that you just read. Your eyes saw the words, but your mind didn't register them.

Every day this is precisely what happens to Maria and Abdul when they are home facing a textbook or a reading on a computer screen. It is time for homework. Maria sees the words, but they don't register. It is as if it were another language. If Maria cannot say the words "fraction," "numerator," and "denominator," then she certainly cannot read them, let alone carry out her fourth grade math assignment. When a biology teacher requests that Abdul review the chapter on mitosis and review the class PowerPoint slides on the topic posted on the teacher's webpage, the assumption is that he can and will read them with care. If he cannot make meaning from the text in the article or on the slides, then the text may as well not be in his hands or present on the website. Unfortunately, many learners who are struggling with words do not ask questions in class because they are self-conscious. Instead of asking their teachers to help them make meaning, they simply watch their teachers talk at them.

Missing: A Pervasive Recognition That Reading Is a Coin with Two Sides

Reading is a coin with two sides. One side is phonemic awareness: the learner's ability to decode the sound-symbol relationship of the written or spoken word. The other side of the coin represents text interaction: the student's ability to make meaning from aural or written text. As Billmeyer (1998, p. 2) points out,

> the meaning of the text is not contained in the words on the page. Instead, the reader constructs meaning by making what she thinks is logical, sensible connection between the new information she reads and what we already know is stored in knowledge frameworks called "schemata."

One of the best sources of evidence that students are interacting with both aural and written text is their notes. Yet taking notes has become something of a farce. Most children view notetaking as copying. It is not active but passive. The magic marker industry made a brilliant move when it generated translucent neon colors. Underlining text has replaced text interaction. We wonder why students retain so little when, in fact, their initial reading and listening experiences are so blatantly superficial. How do we determine that Johnny is listening meaningfully? One of the strongest forms of evidence is in the responses that he creates. A thoughtful review of his notes will tell much about his comprehension.

Despite the fact that reading and writing in the content areas is the bedrock of academic success, it is difficult to locate a university that prepares teachers adequately in reading, writing, speaking, and listening in the content areas. The expectation in teacher preparation programs is that if you are an aspiring math teacher, you will learn how to teach math. The reality is that aspiring math teachers in teaching programs do not learn how to teach Johnny to read math, to discuss it, to understand what he is hearing, and certainly not how to write about math. Underneath the lack of attention to language capacity in teacher education is the message that comprehension is Johnny's problem. Sad to say, the underlying assumption is that Johnny's lack of language capacity is his own, or his English teacher's, problem.

I believe not only that we can move beyond the notion that it is Johnny's problem or the English teacher's problem, but also that we must recognize it is the role of all teachers to be deliberate, relentless, and engaging in building Johnny's communication capacity. What is more, we live in a new time with new tools for supporting his language engagement, with new literacies available.

Missing: An Operational Definition of Digital, Media, and Global Literacies

There is often confusion between the term *technology* hardware and what it is to be literate. The lack of clarity can lead to superficial use of digital tools and quickly made media products of low quality. To be literate is to have depth with making meaning in classical literacy, and the same is true with the new literacies. Without clear definitions of each of the literacies (digital, media, and global) that are translatable into curriculum applications and teaching situations, there is a kind of collusion with superficial usage. In chapter two of our book these three literacies will be unpacked and described.

Missing: Consistent Editing and Revision Strategies—Grades 4–12

In the past, from fourth grade through middle and high school, reading, writing, speaking, and listening skills *were not formally taught and assessed consistently across curriculum areas*. For example, it was rare for teachers in different departments to target specific grammatical conventions and revision techniques to improve the quality of student writing. With the advent of the Common Core State Standards (2010), a key shift has been beginning to buck the trend given that the English Language Arts standards in the CCSS are to be formally taught and developed in all subjects. The change is a slow one, but it is a deliberate attempt to right a problem that still seeps into our schools and systems. Unfortunately, the commonly held view is that this it is still solely the job of the English teacher to support literacy development. Most adolescents need all the help they can get, and, when only one-eighth of their day focuses on the most basic of all of their skills, this is a problem. This view is further compounded by the reality that, by necessity, English teachers spend much of their time on literature. They examine various literary genres, authors, classics, and new voices. Reading skills for literature, which include reading for inference and figurative language, demand specialized teaching, the kind delivered by English teachers. If the average high school English class runs forty minutes a day, five days a week, equaling two hundred minutes, then a realistic estimate is that formal time spent on structures and grammar might be thirty minutes in a week. And this precious little time is undermined when a student also attends a science class, a math class, or even a history or sociology class in which the teacher may or may not care whether a student uses a complete sentence or not.

Missing: Consistent and Ongoing Vertical Planning—Grades K–3

In many individual elementary schools in the United States, inconsistent and competing philosophies of teaching reading plague the early childhood programs, pre-K through grade 3. These tensions create an erratic and piecemeal experience for students. The battle over *whole language* vs. *phonics* has been fierce in our primary grade programs. Compelling arguments can be made for a return to the basic phonics approach and for the opposing holistic camp's use of contextual meaning to motivate learners. But the heart of the problem is the battle itself.

More recent writing on the subject points to the need for a full arsenal of strategies that serve learners from the beginning in their reading programs. The phrase *balanced literacy* emerged as an attempt to represent a resolution to the tension through the philosophy that the whole is the sum of its parts. It is difficult to be critical of a literacy program that is "balanced," just as it would be difficult to be an advocate for "imbalanced" literacy. My review of early childhood curriculum maps indicates that teachers go into their self-contained classrooms and do the best they can without connecting regularly, formally, and vertically for grades K–3. Meetings among grade level teachers may establish a common interpretation of balanced literacy, but this literacy may not be vertically integrated with other grades, even among teachers with the best of training and the best intentions.

As a result, when Johnny moves through elementary school, he is apt to have an uneven journey moving from one teacher who encourages him to "discover" the letter *b* sound in nature and a first grade teacher who tapes the letter to his table or on his shirt as a kind of in-your-face approach. On more than one occasion I have seen angry "reading skirmishes" in elementary schools. Educators care deeply about their beliefs and responsibilities regarding literacy. But if these differences are not resolved, Abdul is likely to be tossed from grade to grade without a careful and seamless building of his emerging language skills. All the while he is getting older and older and outgrowing the short window of opportunity for introducing reading.

There is a particular fascination among children aged three through seven years with sound-symbol relationships, making them responsive to guided instruction about those very relationships. It is only during the first few years of schooling that children like to make letter shapes with clay, that they will say rhyme schemes over and over out loud, and that they will sing made-up melodies to themselves un-self-consciously as they cut out shapes at the table. Sit in any first grade classroom during an open activity period with your eyes closed, and the sounds will astonish you. The rhythmic patterns and flow of vocal inflections create a kind of classroom music. There is the repeated and practiced recitation: "Make the 'b' sound" contrasts with random outbursts from a five-year-old child. But when students are a few years older, much of their spontaneous openness has stopped, and it becomes more difficult to get them to play with the basics of language, even though children, teenagers, and adults have a natural love of language and language play.

With the recent cultivation of the new literacies I believe that the problem of gaps between grade levels and teachers has been exacerbated. Many schools have a "star" digital learning teacher who inserts apps and tools meaningfully into instruction, but for other teachers it is spotty or non-existent. Creating digitally literate, media-savvy, and globally connected learners requires as solid and purposeful a commitment as working through numeracy in a curriculum program.

It is critical that teachers between grade levels and within grade levels collaborate on approaches to reading in these first few years; otherwise, precious time is wasted. We all know how to read. Johnny does not. He will only be four, five, six, and seven years old once.

Missing: Intense and Formal Instruction and Assessment of Speaking and Listening Strategies

Only minimal attention and "lip service" are paid to speaking and listening competencies in any formal fashion in most subjects, creating a schism between the four basic language capacities: reading, writing, listening, and speaking. This separation of the four basic language skills suggests another root problem. One cannot read unless one can say the words out loud. One cannot write unless one can read the words. Listening is the first language capacity developed in the infant. How do we assess listening as a child enters school? All teachers know that there is a big difference between hearing words and listening with engagement. The dearth of opportunities for assessing speaking and listening capacities contrasts dramatically with the many reading and writing assessments. The student who has the confidence and poise to ask a question, provide a detailed response, and find the words to engage in discussion has an enormous advantage. I believe we are not formal enough in our development, monitoring, and expansion of these two human and necessary skills. I have often noted in my workshops with educators that teachers in our educational environment habitually use the four capacities in a stock sequence—reading, writing, speaking, listening—when, in fact, the order should be reversed. As infants we begin by listening, then speaking, then reading, and then we move on to writing.

Most striking as we weave in the new literacies is the opportunity for direct feedback on speaking using media-making tools. Learners can readily see and hear themselves both informally when using a digital tool on their smart phone or in a more sophisticated presentation using iMovie.

In addressing the gaps in classical and contemporary literacies across subject and from grade to grade, I will share strategies that can be adopted realistically by an individual or, even better, by an entire school faculty.

How Can We Develop These Strategies School-Wide?

In many school districts no forum exists for meeting and hammering out skill work both horizontally and vertically. As a result, communication about language skills across disciplines has been hampered. Curriculum guides are often well-intended fictional accounts. They propose what ought to happen in the course of a year with model children, as if all children were moving at a lockstep identical pace. If teachers build their plans on guideline assumptions rather than on what actually occurs, students fall through the cracks.

A key vehicle for integrating these strategies is Curriculum Mapping. The difference between a curriculum *guide* and the curriculum *map* is like the difference between the proposed itinerary and the real trip. Guidelines lay out goals to "guide" our decision making. In contrast, maps document electronically produced document curriculum in real time, reflecting the ground that each teacher actually traverses with the learners through the months of a school year. Data are housed electronically on internet-based software, making the information accessible from any computer at home, in school, or on the road. Through mapping, teachers can find out precisely what is being taught down the hall or in a building across town. They can find what the operational curriculum was in past years. The formidable combination of examining unpacked assessment data with curriculum maps allows us to describe how our learners are performing, how they got there, and what we need to revise in order to improve their performance.

Despite the genuine hope of creating better communication, curriculum committees are often part of the problem. Educators attend far too many meetings with the aim of establishing bureaucratic documents, but these documents do not reflect the realities of what Johnny encounters in the classroom. Teachers in secondary buildings rarely sit together across disciplines to deal with these questions. When they do meet (as in a middle school interdisciplinary team meeting), the conversation usually breaks down into a discussion of the ten most-wanted students. It is not because cross-disciplinary meetings are rare that team meetings degenerate into discussions of problem students. It may be because cross-disciplinary meetings lack the leadership to focus attention on relevant curriculum issues. Educators need to learn how to establish curriculum-based agendas. Curriculum Mapping is detailed as a meaningful and effective tool to address these problems in the last chapter of this book.

The ensuing chapters discuss specific and practical strategies for the classroom teacher that can be integrated into the classroom curriculum. Regarding the institutional level, I propose using Curriculum Mapping as the key tool for integrating the seven strategies consistently throughout the school and on a district level, along with staff development and curriculum revision that will result in demonstrable assessment results in student work. Curriculum Mapping provides a vehicle for addressing the problems presented here and is set up in such a way as to provide flexibility within each specific school setting.

One great gap in the professional preparation of teachers is the provision of strategies for all of us, at all levels and in all subjects, to develop the instructional tools necessary to help all of our students with engaged literacy. That task may seem daunting for a classroom teacher who has not spent time or had training to accommodate language strategies. It may seem like a burden. The strategies that I propose are not meant to be intrusive or to demand adjustments; they are designed to serve as helpful tools that will enable students to become more independent learners. Our students need us to operate always in the present tense. They need good teachers who have the flexibility to work collectively, consistently, and imaginatively to make revisions in their approach to teaching and learning. The seven cross-disciplinary strategies presented here can be employed actively across the curriculum. In the final chapter of the book I show how Curriculum Mapping provides a means of formally documenting these revisions. The outcome will be language-rich environments where each student develops concrete tools to become an independent and engaged learner. Thus in this first chapter I present my case for the first strategy. Teachers need to redefine themselves as language coaches even as they promote the material, concepts, and facts that are the underpinnings of knowledge.

> *Each teacher—at every grade level, in every subject—needs to embrace the notion that he or she is a contemporary literacy teacher.*

1

Updating Roles

Every Teacher Becomes a Contemporary Literacy Teacher

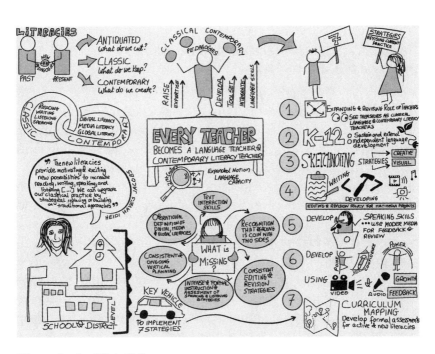

Illustration by Silvia Tolisano

Language capacity is the root of all learning experiences. Whether it is listening to directions, reading a passage, writing a response, or discussing a point of view, the individual student's ability to perform and grow in a classroom rests squarely on his or her corresponding language capacity. However, the 21st century has expanded the notion of language capacity, requiring the focused attention of educators. Now the very concept of "classroom" has evolved dramatically, and with that shift there is an increased necessity for rich language capacity. Reaching into a pocket and pulling up a *smart* device is akin to reaching for a classroom. Whether a student is texting a friend, sharing music on Cimbal, transmitting a moment via Instagram, checking background on Wikipedia, or Skyping with a friend in Japan, learning has shifted. An entering kindergarten child is most likely to be highly familiar and agile in touch and effect interactions on an iPad, savvy with a smart board, and creating video interactions on the app Get-Puppet. What are the implications for these shifts on scaffolding literacy?

New Pedagogy: The Relationship Between Past and Present Literacies

In order to get a handle on how life has changed in education settings and what those changes mean to literacy, let us examine the fundamental shift in pedagogy because of the startling shift in access to information, media, and social communication. I and my colleague Marie Alcock and focus the critical discussion about the shift in roles and relationships between teacher and learners into three pedagogical camps (2017, p. 11). Each of these pedagogies directly responds to three ongoing questions regarding curriculum, instruction, and assessment that educators need to address in order to be responsive to our learners: What do we cut? What do we keep? What do we create? In addition to describing the three pedagogies, there are comments regarding the inference for our focus on literacy.

> **Antiquated pedagogy (What do we cut?):** There is no direct relationship between teacher and learner, but rather the

emphasis here is on the dispensing of knowledge to the student who is a receptacle. The word "coverage" comes to mind when we consider that content is to be presented and that it is the child's problem to memorize and make sense out of it. Therefore, literacy is equated with the ability of students to listen and to read without a great deal of concern for their response in any depth. This antiquated notion also tends to minimize the necessity for teacher intervention into the development of a literate learner. The notion behind this stance is basically "a child either reads or does not, there is not much a teacher can do about it, thus, let us sort those who cannot read into more menial types of work." Through most of human history that approach has ruled the lives of human beings, given that the concept of universal education only began as a viable approach in the latter part of the 19th century.

Classical pedagogy (What do we keep?): Classical traditions are timeless, thus always timely. When we think of great classic works of literature, art, architecture, or science, a culture acknowledges the critical role that meaningful thought and engagement play from any period of history. With classical pedagogy there is a powerful and clear relationship between teacher and learner regarding the best way to pose content, provoke questioning, organize learning groups, and observe student needs. In terms of literacy, the critical role of an interactive teacher posing the right questions, calling attention to tips to assist the emerging reader, modeling good listening, providing sentence starters to pose questions, encouraging risk taking in writing that first original sentence, and applauding progress is essential and will always be essential as timeless teaching pedagogy. Classical literacy is predicated on the cultivation of the basic four capacities: reading, writing, speaking, and listening. These capacities are timeless, timely, and necessary. Throughout the book there will be suggested strategies to support four capacities and their inherent connections. The contention here is that the new literacies sit on the shoulders of these classical approaches.

If a child cannot read, he or she cannot read a computer screen.

Contemporary pedagogy (What do we create?) With learning 24/7 as a possibility and the extraordinary immediacy of net-based tools, we have new kinds of learners. Our children and youth are self-navigators who can reach out and "browse" sources freely and with ease. However, this does not mean they are literate in their searching. Accessing is not the same as diving deep and making strategic selections of quality information and resources. As teachers in our 21st-century times, we need to cultivate new approaches that support learners in engaging in the new literacies: digital, media, and global in conjunction with the classical. To clarify what these literacies look like in classroom life and what their connection is to the classical literacies, I have developed a definition of each grounded in what they look like in educative practice based. To be clear, each of the literacies is distinctive from the others, though there are points of overlapping. I will share my working definitions of these key literacies below.

Digital literacy is "the proficiency to effectively employ web-based applications, internet-based tools, and repository sites to further meaningful research and development." It is predicated on the development of four capabilities (Jacobs, 2014, p. 7):

Accessing capability, which is the ability of the learner to enter the portal into web-based learning and applications. There are currently three points of access: key-boarding, voice, and touch and effect. It is important to note the similarity between phonemic awareness in classical literacy and accessing capability, because neither skill set guarantees literacy. Simply because I can decode a word does not make me a knowledge, insightful, or meaning-making reader. Similarly, simply accessing the internet does not guarantee that I have any sophistication. This latter point leads us to the next capability.

Selection capability is about strategic and informed choice regarding the location of the appropriate digital tool, application or website resource to match the demands of a problem or issue. Given the ease and immediacy of digital tools, it is tempting to take the first tool or the first website that appears. In the classical world of print, this is akin to simply taking the first book that appears in a library.

Curation capability is a skill set focused on the critical need to organize source material and to display that information effectively in a virtual format. Just as a museum curator organizes the display and sequence of paintings, the web-based curator shows an intelligent sense of what resources are of value by creating a clearinghouse of sources. The skill of "tagging" key sites and applications is central to creating a website reference tool.

Creation capability points to solution and product building using digital tools, such as creating an application, software platform, or model employing virtual tools.

Media Literacy is the response to and creation of media forms of communication. Going beyond the classical formats for communication of written, print, and oral traditions, educators are adding the newer forms of the last century and our current one. Whether film, video, radio, or audio cast, the necessity for healthy criticism of what we take in is central to becoming a literate and sophisticated recipient of information and imaginative experience. Likewise, the ability to create works of media necessitates specific skills for meaningful and technically proficient outcomes. I choose to organize this literacy around two capabilities: receptive and generative (Jacobs, 2014, p. 8):

Receptive media capability points to a critical review of both information and narrative media formats. Students can validate informational source material. One of the most important skills here is the ability of students to avoid taking the first site that comes up when using a browser to search for information on the internet. They literally can identify the perspective or angle that is taken, such as what the cameraman holds that determines what the viewer sees in a news report. Information is gathered from television and film on an unprecedented level because of access to media via a computer, tablet, or smart phone. If the media is narrative as in film, the goal is to cultivate media critics who value the story telling, direction, acting performances, craft, and technical expertise that are requisite in great film and the consummate talent of great filmmakers. Just as students study literary authors, so should our students be studying auteurs.

Generative media capability is the ability to express personal messages or stories through media formats. The world of "filmmaking" has been democratized through the 21st century with the ease of access to media-making tools, whether it is a video cast or audio cast. Any laptop is akin to a production studio. There is a tremendous range of choices available to learners with the technical ability and motivation to create media, yet simply using a digital camera on a smart phone does not assure quality. The teaching profession needs to improve professional development skills to help educators become more generative in developing media in order to support our learners.

Global Literacy is focused on expanding both the perspective of learners to relate to people and places throughout the world and the technical skills to locate them. Clearly this literacy goes beyond the traditional notion that "this is social studies," but rather that is an interdisciplinary reality. Building upon the fundamental geography skill sets that are now possible using digital applications ranging from Google Earth to GPS tools, students can directly connect with real people in real places in real time using Skype or Google Hangout. The basis for global literacy, that is, making meaning about the world are four global competencies found in *the Global Competency Matrix* developed over several years by a working task force supported by CCSSO and the Asia Society (Jackson and Boix-Mansilla, 2011). It was my good fortune to work on this task force, and I believe that these four fundamental competencies that emerged are imminently practical and curriculum friendly. They are:

- ◆ Investigate the World;
- ◆ Recognize Perspectives;
- ◆ Communicate Ideas;
- ◆ Take Action

What is more, I would encourage teachers to include the following: "the prefix, GEO, becomes a curriculum turn-key here when attached to the full array of subjects in the curriculum: GEO-literature; GEO-politics; GEO-economics; GEO-arts. Thus, the globally literate student is led to study contemporary issues that are by their very nature interdisciplinary with sustainability issues at the forefront" (Jacobs, 2014, p. 9).

In keeping with our discussion about linking classical literacy to the new literacies, global literacy or global competence directly provides opportunities for necessary communication. The ability to listen thoughtfully and to speak and to communicate with others is central to becoming a global citizen, if not a student of the world.

Examining the emergence of new pedagogy linked to new literacies raises this critical question: What is the role for the contemporary teacher in supporting modern literate learners?

The Classical and Contemporary Literacies in Every Classroom

Both the classical reading, writing, speaking, and listening strategies and the contemporary new literacies cut across disciplines. In the world of formal education, these strategies are requisite at every level for Johnny, Maria, Abdul, and Rachel. The need to read, write, speak, and listen effectively is fundamental to every subject, in every grade, and in every class these learners will ever attend. What is more, these very foundational literacies are requisite for moving into the new literacies.

The fulfillment of this need is complicated by standards, whether they are Common Core, content specific, as in Next Generation Science Standards, or specifically developed at the state level. This complication exists because standards that are written are tied to grade level standardization. Thus, there is an "as if" presumption. I have often thought that the adverb *independently* should be added to the end of every benchmark and standard, because ultimately Johnny is on his own. Rigid instructional adherence to standards is implemented if all children are fluent in standard English. It should be no surprise when test scores plummet in a school. Every standardized test, whether it is state or national, is first and foremost a *reading* test. If Johnny can't read the math problems, then he cannot complete them accurately. Explanations of mathematical procedures and principles are written in sentences and with polysyllabic words. If he cannot comprehend basic prompts like "select" or "summarize" or "determine," then he will fail on the test item. Johnny's difficulties with comprehension arise not only from his unfamiliarity with simple fundamental words; they are compounded by the fact that explanations of mathematical procedures and principles are written with precise terminology. The preeminence of high-stakes testing adds even more pressure to the lives of our children and to our teachers. The so-called move to "technology-based" testing in general is simply moving the paper version of multiple choice to an electronic format. Students still need to read these tests without anyone's help.

Elementary school teachers launch children into a world of words by devoting hours of instruction to increasing their language skills. Knowing there is a narrow window of opportunity to get our youngest learners off and running, these teachers feel enormous pressure. Secondary school teachers rely heavily on their students' ability to bring home reading material at night, whether on a website or in textbook, and to carry out homework. Middle and high school teachers often deal with over a hundred students in a day, and they base their assignments on the assumption that the students *can* read and react to the text. Teachers are very dependent on each other to build and sustain these fundamental tools. Academic literacy in our public and private schools is a K–12 problem. It is critical to revisit the role of the teacher and the way teachers communicate with each other about their learners. To be crystal clear, standards may come and go, but there will always be an unrelenting need to develop a learner's language capacity in order to function in the world and have a meaningful life.

Every Teacher Is a Communications Coach

If you are an eighth grade math teacher, then you are a speech teacher. If Johnny cannot describe in conversation with you what confuses him in computing an algebraic equation, then he will be a frustrated learner. He needs practice with oral explanations in math, or he will *become* a child left behind. He needs practice in listening to you and knowing how to ask a clarifying question. He may be using conversational language rather than academic language, referring to the denominator as the "bottom thing" and the numerator as the "top thing"; he may refer to mathematical operations using imprecise language, muddling mathematical thinking in his own mind. He is only thirteen and self-conscious. How can you help him speak and listen thoughtfully?

If you are a third grade teacher presenting your social studies unit on Japan, then you are clearly a writing teacher. Maria needs your help. She is trying to convey her point of view about how the fact that Japan is an island affects people there. Her writing seems clichéd. You know it, and so does she. How can you coach her to choose very specific words that will make her writing come alive? How can you help her write and reread her work? She needs an academic inventory of words that will help her think in the language of social studies.

If you are a high school physics teacher and you rely heavily on student lab reports, you must teach your students how to employ an empirical style of writing. Abdul might say "this" when he needs to say "that." Now the majority of your 120 students write labs as if they are doing you a favor. The labs look copied—not the thorough response you had hoped for. Rather than getting angry with your students, perhaps you need to help them with notetaking. Do they even know what makes a note noteworthy? They need your help.

You are a physical education teacher working with kindergarten students, and their ability to listen carefully to your directions will affect their actual safety. If Rachel doesn't understand your words but just smiles at you, she cannot progress. Listening capability is critical to her success on the playing field. She needs to demonstrate her understanding of your coaching words on the playing field and in the gym. In the best sense of classical literacy, every teacher is a language teacher.

Now . . . the Connection From Classical to Contemporary

The case that will be made in this book is that the new literacies provide motivating and exciting new possibilities to increase reading, writing, speaking, and listening. Rather than classical literacies being at odds with the new, *they are mutually dependent*. We can *upgrade* our classical practice by strategically replacing or building on traditional approaches (Jacobs, 2010). Let us reconsider the four examples in the previous section. Johnny's eighth grade math teacher can assist him with listening by providing a link to a Khan Academy Video on Linear Equations, encouraging Johnny to replay it and to generate a list of questions to be recorded on his iPad using PhotoBooth. Maria, our third grader working on the Japan unit, can cultivate vocabulary independently using Visual Thesaurus. Abdul's need for notetaking and notemaking strategies can be enhanced by employing a visual notetaking tool like Paper by 53.

An example of the marriage of classical and contemporary literacy is in the dynamic application Newsela. In this application, newspaper articles are selected because of their relevance to students at different ages. The key function is that the article can have the Lexile level adjusted to match the reading level of the student. In short, a class always has a range of readers, and a teacher can immediately differentiate to match that level. Figure 1.1 shows that the reading level is set at a 560L but could be adjusted to 1120L or MAX with more demanding vocabulary and sentence structure.

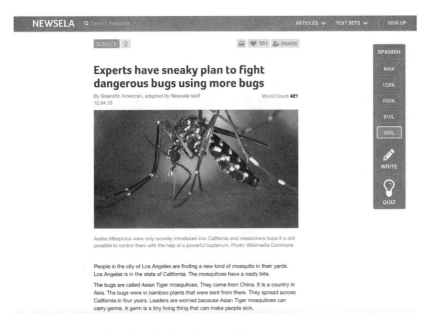

FIGURE 1.1 Example of lexile levels from Newsela.com

The Media Savvy/Media Making: Learner and Teacher

Our modern media is not a new 21st-century enterprise, but is rooted in photography and recording from the 19th century into film, television, and radio into the 20th century. Yet there is a curriculum drought in our classrooms for more consistent integration of formal film viewing and media production. Certainly we can integrate "the moving image" more strategically into our curriculum plans to cultivate "savvy" viewers of media. Just as we have created a wealth of resources directed toward a set of canonical books for formal study in our schools in order to develop sophistication and taste in our emerging readers, so should we do the same with film and television media viewing. Frank W. Baker and I discuss the need for developing a film canon (Jacobs and Baker, 2014, p. 68). The formal study of film and television based on critical analysis derives from the identical root of critical print analysis. Arguably it is a universal tenet subscribed to by teachers that the careful analysis of great literary works not only fosters a depth of appreciation of the work itself but also leads to potentially greater writing skill. High schools students dissect the works of F. Scott Fitzgerald, Langston Hughes, and Harper Lee to study superb craft and timeless message, but there is also the hope that they will absorb the lessons of powerful writers to apply to their own attempts at self-expression. In this same spirit, modern teachers can bridge these classical views of print and connect them to the formal study of media. Frank and I developed the Film Canon Project (www.filmcanonproject.com) to provide and model an archive where quality narrative, documentary, and animated films can be listed with links as potential source material for curriculum planning. As we examine the connections between print and media, a direct bridge is having students directly study screenplays as they view great film works. On our Film Canon Project website under resources there exists a wonderful list of free downloadable screenplays of wonderful films nominated for Academy Awards. The possibilities are tremendous for engaging students in reading the actual text from a screenplay and then seeing how a director brings it to life on the screen. In short, reading is encouraged and accentuated by bridging the two mediums.

If students become better judges of quality media, they will likely generate better quality productions. Certainly media-making possibilities have grown exponentially with the extraordinary growth of applications and platforms available on our laptops. In a very real way, a teacher is now a video producer, and the students are on the "movie lot" shooting film, editing, introducing sound, and then screening their work online or on an LCD projector. I encourage teachers to improve their personal expertise using one or two tools at a time to increase their comfort with media making. We have provided on our Curriculum 21 Clearinghouse (curriculum21.com/clearinghouse) a tag titled *Media Sharing*, which provides a wide array of tools ranging from Animoto to Screenflow to VoiceThread that can be employed by learners to share their ideas in new media formats. To make the connection between classical literacy approaches, I encourage teachers to have student storyboard and layout their production first, as well as script any voice-over components to a presentation. There is a frequent red flag rightfully raised by teachers who are concerned that students will run around with their digital devices, quickly shoot a video clip, and proceed to throw it onto YouTube in a superficial manner. Editing is required in any composition to build quality and nuance. The classical approach to review and revision in writing carries over directly to media making in all subjects and courses.

News Sources: Fake Versus Authentic

Wrestling with current news is proving to be a timely issue confronting teachers that merges classical and contemporary literacies. When viewing media, whether an online newspaper, Facebook post, video clip, organization website, or blog post, our students are barraged with images and words. The necessity to discern what is factual material from authentic and legitimate sources has become a genuine necessity. What is more, the need to assist students in distinguishing presentation of information from interpretation of information is palpable. Given the power of the image, bias is amplified on what the screen shows us and literally from what angle. In her summary of strategies for debunking fake news, *Truth, Truthiness, Triangulation: A News Literacy Tool Kit for the "Post-Truth" Era*, Joyce Valenza (2016) lists key active literacy approaches:

- ◆ Check About and About Me pages
- ◆ Interrogate URLs
- ◆ Suspect the sensational
- ◆ Go back to the source
- ◆ Go back to the story again (and again)
- ◆ Think outside the reliability box
- ◆ Triangulate by using a hoax-tracker such as Snopes.com
- ◆ Determine the genre of the piece
- ◆ Check your own search attitude and biases
- ◆ Use a little energy

- ◆ Stop before you forward (or use)
- ◆ Be suspicious of pictures

What I find particularly striking about Valenza's list and the blog post itself is the direct connection between classical literacy and the modern formats teachers need to bridge. The classical approach to critical reading of print has been a critical component of classical instruction in all of our subject areas. We want our students to challenge sources and to seek reliable information in all forms of communication.

Global Perspectives: Classical and Contemporary

As teachers open the windows of our classrooms and let perspectives from the other side of town or the other side of the world pour into modern learning environments, it is critical that we expand language capacities even as we expand perspectives. Whether through point-to-point communications, a Skype global book group, or a foreign film, our new literacies give us a platform for engaging students in taking another point of view. Yet the classical tradition of listening and speaking, the bedrock of a good interview, holds true as the anchor for a quality webcast respecting the culture of the interviewee. The link between the classical and contemporary is central to becoming a literate global citizen in every classroom. Middle school literature classes might share a global book study on *The Giver* by Lois Lowry with students in another part of the country or the world. Second graders in Connecticut are comparing the on-time records of trains at Union Station in New Haven with their counterparts at a school near Shibuya Station, Tokyo, Japan. Physical education teachers connect their students to explore the underlying reasons that different sports are valued more in some parts of the world than in others. Throughout the book, I hope to share specific strategies for cultivating globally aware and informed students through active literacy.

Teachers can deliberately connect classical and contemporary literacies to cultivate and to empower engaged learners.

2

Developing Three Types of Words with Classical Approaches and Digital Tools

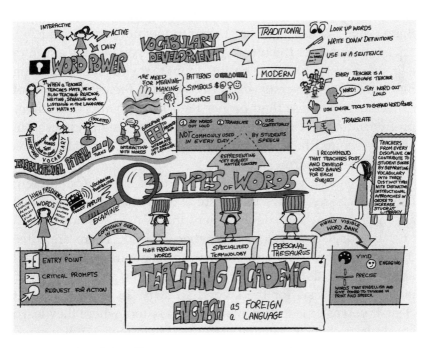

Illustration by Silvia Tolisano

There is one class where each and every student speaks out loud every day, one class where every student is expected to use correct grammar in speech, one class where the learner is given words and uses them, one class where pronunciation, enunciation, and inflection are requisite: This class is foreign language. When students learn a new language, they get the best type of literacy instruction. I recommend that English should be taught as if it were a foreign language in all of our subjects. A key feature of language instruction is the development of word power—actively, interactively, and daily in world language classes. Walk into any French, Spanish, Mandarin, Japanese, or Italian language class, and you will hear the teacher asking students to speak out loud. If you walk into Mr. Mendez's Spanish class, you hear students repeating words. They say them aloud; they attempt to say them properly; they employ them in a context; and they learn to speak Spanish **properly**. Think of how absurd it would be if Mr. Mendez said: "Watch me. Listen to me speak Spanish, but don't say anything out loud. Quiet over there while I speak Spanish! Listen to me; now try to read."

Let us consider the word "properly." If you were to enroll in a French class, could there be any doubt that you will be learning high level French versus slang or idiomatic French? We do not expect anything less than proper French usage and vocabulary pronunciation, yet when it comes to the way English is used in our classrooms, the low standard for even basic communication is too often the norm.

Careful observation of the methods of world (or foreign) language classes shows that there is a distinctive instructional approach to language development that contrasts sharply with how language is developed in other subjects. There are three distinctive types of vocabulary with corresponding instructional approaches. This pattern for organizing and delivering word power is the basis for the second strategy. To make the point clear, if you ask most students in a high school where they learn vocabulary, chances are that they say it is in their English class. But vocabulary is not learned best in English class alone. If it is acquired and deployed in all other subjects, the student has a genuine opportunity to build the ultimate language power tool: an internalized vault of words. On any major standardized test, the subtest that is the best predictor of overall success is vocabulary. Obviously, the student who has developed a command of words and can make sense of those words in a range of contexts has the best chance of reading, writing, speaking, and listening in any situation. In a detailed analysis of vocabulary development, as E. D. Hirsch (2013) notes:

> There's a positive correlation between a student's vocabulary size in grade 12, the likelihood that she will graduate from college, and her future level of income. The reason is clear: vocabulary size is a convenient proxy for a whole range of educational attainments and abilities—not just skill in reading, writing, listening, and speaking but also general knowledge of science, history, and the arts.

In short, words matter. To incentivize student pursuit of word strength we see the timely convergence of digital tools to assist with vocabulary development.

In the spirit of our first chapter, the deliberate integration of contemporary tools enhances the cultivation of vocabulary development for all three tiers. When examining the three different types of words, let us set up an expanded toolkit employing contemporary digital applications to assist teachers and learners in expanding their vocabulary possibilities.

Down with Simply Looking Up Words

The traditional approach to improving student performance with vocabulary development is based on asking students to "look up words," write down the definitions, and then use them in a sentence. Copying words from a dictionary is passive, so there are glaring problems with this model. Each word hangs in suspended animation and remains out of context among twenty random, and usually unattached, words on a list. Most often, the students *never say the word aloud in class*. What is more, there are new possibilities for digital engagement that can instruct and reinforce better language usage.

Look at the way a world (foreign) language teacher builds vocabulary. Mr. Sanchez presents words in situational clusters that help students focus on employing words in real contexts: "This week we are going to study marketplace words. On Friday, we will simulate a walk through a Seville marketplace across from the Alfonso Palace." Students are expected not only to say the words aloud but also to use them in sentences and employ them in simulated situations. In short, they are expected to speak to each other and to the teacher. Everyone speaks in Spanish. It is surprising that we do not use this technique in English classes. Foreign language instructors tend not to take any sets of words for granted. Everyday words or high-frequency words are reviewed as well as more specific types of contextually based words. Finally, world language teachers praise the additional initiative shown when a student inserts a richer, more colorful word into an assignment, whether written or spoken. All instructors could learn from language teachers: in a sense, when a teacher teaches math, he or she is also teaching reading, writing, speaking, and listening in the language of math. What is more, we now have new digital media tools to expand the opportunities for students to independently grow their word power.

World language teachers often use modern media formats to reinforce what students hear in context by having students watch films from other countries with, and then without, subtitles. The ability of the student to stop the action in a film narrative, replay the scene, and then speak the dialogue out loud is a longstanding world language approach. What if English teachers had students follow films with the screenplay in hand, stop the action, and have the students repeat the words aloud? The ability to say unfamiliar and new words in context is a key to language development.

Grouping Words Into Distinctive Types and Employing Digital Tools

Research on reading indicates the value of strategic grouping of words (Stall and Nagy, 2005). Grouping words strategically contrasts with the more common practice of clumping all words into one big vocabulary pile. Another specific approach with three tiers identifies a level of basic words that the learner has cultivated at home, high frequency words across a range of domains employed by mature language users and highly focused content specific words.

(Beck, McCoweon, and Kukan, 2013)

To achieve a major shift in the way we teach language so that it is a powerful tool in all subjects, I proposed to build vocabulary in three distinctive arenas in the first edition of this book and still hold with this notion, with one caveat. The third tier formerly was called "embellishments," and I have elected to rename it "personal power words":

1. High-frequency words
2. Specialized terminology
3. Personal word thesaurus

The three categories are chosen because students can understand what they mean and can sort words accordingly at any age. Each vocabulary arena should be developed with three corresponding and distinctive approaches. We should explain the three types of words clearly in every subject, K–12, with the goal that students learn to translate each type of vocabulary into their own words, just as students of French or Japanese do habitually. I am suggesting that students learn to translate academic English into their own vernacular and then to employ the academic terms with the same facility.

Employing new visual and auditory digital tools can assist learners to independently engage in expanding their facility. There are visual tools such as Visuword (see Figure 2.1) that not only provide a clear definition but also graphically display word relationships and variations immediately in a way that is often easier for a student to grasp than merely reading the definition:

Some Basics

To appreciate the need for this tripartite approach, let us look at some basics about the act of reading. Reading is composed of two related components: phonemic awareness and text interaction (Billmeyer, 1998). To develop phonemic awareness, the

FIGURE 2.1 Example of the power of interactive vocabulary building with VISUWORDS.com

reader must be able to make sound patterns that relate to the symbol pattern in written text. For example, when Maria sees a deliberate shape on the page, such as the letter "b" in English, she can register the name of the symbol and, more importantly, link it to a sound pattern. In other words, she can hear it. She then can reproduce that sound externally, or orally. Maria proceeds to register the link between symbol and sound internally in her mind, and eventually she will display the sound in writing. Maria has a distinctive and deliberate awareness of the phonemic pattern. But the act of matching symbol to sound, *decoding*, is not actually reading in the sense that *reading* is an act of making meaning from the patterns of symbols and sound. Nevertheless, the awareness of phonemic pattern is necessary for Maria to move to the ultimate purpose of interacting with the text. This component represents the ability of the reader to find and make meaning from the words. It is not just that Maria can reproduce the sound patterns she sees, but that when these patterns are linked together to make words, she can gather sense and purpose.

Deriving meaning from text is personal interaction. It is the heart of reading. In the compelling book *Mosaic of Thought* (2007), Zimmermann and Keene discuss the ultimately intimate and personal nature of creating meaning from text. Through their readers' workshop model they wanted to create the opportunity to fill the gap that was too often a part of the reading experiences which they and so many of us had in our elementary and secondary schools. That gap stems from the reader's inability to interact personally with the text and create meaning from it; thus, learner cultivated strategies are key. As the authors state:

> Remember—the strategies are tools. They are a means to an end—comprehension—not an end in themselves. Our goal is to help children become avid readers who look forward to a time alone with a great book in hand.
>
> (p. 43)

If you have ever attempted to learn a new language as an adult, then you know what I mean by the relationship between recognizing sounds and making meaning from them. It can be daunting to respond to and recognize new sounds and new symbols, especially in languages using alphabets different from one's own. It is thrilling to begin to grasp those basic phonemes as words emerge both aurally and in text. Yet it is not enough to simply reproduce the sound pattern. Only when Maria comprehends and interacts with the text can she claim it for her own. Central then to her growing language capacity is her arsenal of words. The more words we "own," the more likely we are to make meaning aurally and textually. Having recently begun to take Spanish language lessons, I am particularly aware, as a novice, that I possess only a handful of words to employ, so almost everything I hear when I listen to fluent Spanish speakers goes right by me. I just don't have the words. It is humbling.

An Instructional Pitfall: Heaping Vocabulary

It is confusing to learners (and to teachers) when *vocabulary* is lumped into an instructional heap. If I were to ask most youngsters what "vocabulary" means in school, they would likely respond, "New words that I don't know and will never use, but that I will need on a test or someplace." When handed a list of vocabulary words, some learners certainly have the capacity to look up meanings and then put them into a sentence, eventually recalling what these words mean. But, frankly, most students do not have this capability. We should segregate words into groups that promote the easiest ways for them to be learned and integrated into the world of the learner. Such a technique is comparable to how a physical education teacher separates general warm-up exercises, specific drills, and then the game. The game synthesizes the first two strategies in a sophisticated way so that the player finesses the finer points of the game. Similarly, the music teacher starts with warm-up exercises on scales and rehearsing sections of pieces before tackling an actual performance.

High-Frequency Words

The most basic types of words that teachers provide for learners are high-frequency words. These are the entry words that are commonly seen in all manner of texts and life situations. If we are planning a trip to France, our guidebook has commonly used words and phrases featured prominently at the beginning of the text: "Where is . . . ; How much . . . ; left, right, straight, yes, no." With practice, these frequent phrases help us make our way through the charming streets of Aix-en-Provence. We can make change in euros, find a cheese shop, and locate a hotel (instead of buy one).

Young learners in early childhood classes easily recognize high-frequency words visually. When these words become an assimilated part of the reading function, sounding out is not necessary because there is an almost automatic response. The reader employs a kind of shorthand with words such as *say, go, was, is, that, there, here, we, look,* and *the.* Primary grade teachers and foreign language teachers post these words prominently for reference and support. High-frequency words that are verbs are critical prompts or requests for action, e.g., *tell, show, explain, draw.* Rachel's first grade teacher, Mr. Evans, has these words prominently displayed. You can imagine what would happen if he were to turn to his six-year-old students and say, "I'm taking these words down. You're old enough to know them. And while I'm at it, I'm taking down the alphabet." Yet this is precisely what happens to Rachel within a very few years.

We make huge assumptions about these types of words as Rachel enters fourth or fifth grade, and we make even more assumptions as she reaches secondary school. We assume, for instance, that our learners continue assimilating these words without conscious, deliberate support in each and every subject and classroom. One of the most striking studies that grabbed my attention many years ago on this subject appeared in the *NASSP Bulletin* (Barton, 1997). It reports that 35% of all achievement test errors were fundamental reading errors. If Rachel cannot translate the directions independently, she will not be able to take any test on any testing day without her teacher. The core prompt in the test item points the student in the direction of the task itself.

As teachers we use high-frequency words constantly in class, assuming that the students are "with us" and that they understand the meaning of these common words. From about the fourth grade onward, we assume that students understand protocols or request words. These words are the real demons in reading, and when students have problems with them, they are the source of enormous frustration. As students get older, they are expected to work at home alone and to have an engaged relationship with their textbooks. We assume that Maria has an understanding of the nature of an assignment, the meaning of the textbook, and a clear idea of what is expected. However, when she takes tests, the high-frequency words often throw her off course. It is analogous to assuming that we can independently navigate the streets of Aix-en-Provence without any firm knowledge of the basics. The foreign language teacher never takes these words for granted and, more to the point, constantly translates the words in speech, reading, writing, and listening. It is central to Rachel's reading independence that she eventually can translate important prompts without teacher intervention. On testing day she will have to go it alone.

Here are some examples of high-frequency words:

analyze	estimate	organize
cite	examine	paraphrase
comment	expand	persuade
compare	explain	peruse
consider	explore	prove
contrast	extract	reason
create	find	recover
define	flow chart	recreate
design	generate	redesign
detail	identify	refer
determine	imagine	reflect
develop	inject	refrain
diagram	insert	refuse
discern	interpret	reject
discover	investigate	research
discuss	justify	revise
display	legitimize	select
dissuade	limit	set priorities

edit	locate	solve
elaborate	marginalize	state
eliminate	match	summarize
embellish	measure	support
establish	obtain	unpack

High-frequency words appear again and again for students. What is critical is that Johnny has a ready paraphrase. Students should carry a list of such words in their materials with corresponding paraphrases: "What's another word for 'select'?" the teacher asks. "Choose" or "pick" is the response.

A middle school teacher in Florida once told me about an eye-opening conversation with her son, who attended the same school where she teaches. He complained that all of his teachers assumed he was "smart" because his mother was a teacher. He confided that sometimes he didn't know "what the words mean" and said, "I never have really understood the difference between compare and contrast." She said she was surprised, yet not really "so surprised" because, in retrospect, when she thought about it, the many students in her class who nod as though they understand might not really understand.

A critical and important task for classroom teachers to carry out is item analysis of tests. Look for the prompts to see if there are patterns of words that might be sending students in the wrong direction, not only as they complete tests but also as they carry out assignments. It is important to remember that when students take tests, they are doing so as independent readers. Consider the following examples of test item prompts that students missed because of their misunderstanding of the high-frequency word:

◆ Second Grade Math
   Test item: Freddie has five coins in his pocket. The coins add up to 66 cents. Explain or show the coins Freddie might have in his pocket.
   Misunderstood prompt: Many of the students had difficulty understanding what the test item required of them because the word *explain* was an unfamiliar term. In

this instance, some students thought that the prompt was asking them to choose which directive was the correct response, *explaining* or *showing in pictures*.

◆ Third Grade Social Studies

Test item: After examining the rainfall chart and the map of Hawaii, draw conclusions about the type of animals and plants that will grow there.

Misunderstood prompt: Many students literally "drew" their conclusions.

◆ Seventh Grade Biology

Test item: Distinguish the difference between flora and fauna in a paragraph.

Misunderstood prompt: Many students thought "distinguish" meant "extinguish."

◆ Tenth Grade English Literature

Test item: After reading the two reviews of Harper Lee's *To Kill a Mockingbird*, opine on the bias of the reviewers in a written paragraph.

Misunderstood prompt: "Opine" is a verb that probably no high school student in history has ever used voluntarily.

When students return with homework that indicates a misunderstanding of the directions, it is likely that their response to the task verb was a key reason for the misunderstanding. It is easy to assume that students are not listening or paying attention; in fact, they may not clearly understand the words in the directions. One reason students struggle with high-frequency words is that they do not use them in their own daily speech. I cannot imagine a middle or high school student declaring, "Determine the reason for our disagreement!" or "Infer the meaning of the blockage of my locker" or "Synthesize the characteristics of our assorted cliques. Oh, and provide supportive details in your answer." The point is that we understand the words we actually use in our ongoing communication. If students do not employ these words, then they will not understand them, especially in high-stress testing situations. Yet we expect students to be fluent in language that is significantly different from their vernacular speech. This is why students need to learn to translate words from their speech to the academic register. One characteristic of students who perform well on standardized or criteria-referenced tests is, in fact, their ability to assimilate high-frequency protocols with ease.

As previously noted, the development of high-frequency words is an intensive priority in early childhood classes, but it seems to end abruptly around grade four. One reason for this halt is the heavy content demands of upper elementary education. Unless a child is identified as "at risk," diminished attention to high-frequency vocabulary occurs. If a child is a middle- to low-range reader, the problem is exacerbated. Upper elementary school children are expected to read more and more on their own, to listen more intently, and to understand all that the teacher presents to them. Directive tasks commence with verbs that become more abstract as the child moves on to more complex thinking. As the elementary child proceeds into middle level education, where a teacher has five times the number of students in a day, the demands on receptive language capacities increase.

HFW Virtual Notebook

The key strategy here is for teachers to ask students to keep a set of student-developed and personal translations for high-frequency words—words that they encounter in class, on the blackboard, on charts, and so on—in a virtual notebook. The student's paraphrase should be made in a different font color. In an interactive platform such as Google Forms, as shown in Figure 2.2, each student can personally target HFW (High Frequency Words) that are problematic for them.

As adults who have college teaching degrees, we find it easy to blatantly condescend to our students: "Well, of course, they understand these words." Yet I would ask us to think about how foolish a child of ten or thirteen or seventeen might feel if he or she has to request clarification about the most fundamental of words explained. "What do *compare* and *contrast* mean?" is not asked by students in classrooms. Students would feel stupid and silly doing it, although these are the very words that many of them need. Furthermore, these basic

My High Frequency Words

* Required

Here is a HFW that I am working on. *

| reasons |

Here is my definition of the word.

| The ideas that tell why something happened or why something should happen |

Here is a HFW that I am working on

| determine |

Here is my definition of the word.

| Think about, then make the best choice |

Submit

Never submit passwords through Google Forms.

FIGURE 2.2 Example of possible use of Google Forms for a student to identify high frequency words needing development

words sometimes have different denotations and connotations in various classrooms; hence, the word *solve* in math class might mean something quite different in an English class: "Did Holden solve his dilemma?"

As students enter the upper elementary grades and move on into secondary school, they face ever increasing language challenges. The language becomes more abstract, and more independent reading is expected. In addition, teachers make more assumptions about what the students comprehend. Because teachers have greater numbers of students and more complex and voluminous content to address, they have less time to devote to language development. As a result, explicit instruction in reading strategies diminishes unless the student receives special education services.

Specialized Terminology

Vocabulary that focuses on highly contextualized applications in specific fields or disciplines is identified as *specialized terminology*. These words and phrases are not used commonly among students in everyday speech, but they are certainly employed with regularity among specialists in a field. Specialized terms describe concepts or ideas that require definition in a context. For example, the term *photosynthesis* is a specialized term used in the field of biology. The term *oligarchy* is specific to social studies.

Teachers often explain specialized terminology to students, using each term fluently and with clarity in the course of the explanation. But it is only in the rare classroom that each and every student is expected to say the word aloud, translate its meaning actively, and then use it both orally and contextually in writing. The problem goes back to the initial contention of this chapter that there is much to be gained by using strategies of the foreign language teacher. Students in a foreign language class say the words out loud, translate them, and use them contextually. For example, Ms. Momiji is working with her students in a Japanese language class on specialized words dealing with travel: *passport, airlines, high-speed trains, visa, currency, shrine, temple,* and so forth. The students practice and demonstrate the use of the words in a context as they simulate planning a trip to Kyoto. While continually working on her students' proper pronunciation and usage, Ms. Momiji also directs her students to use these words actively in dialogue and in writing. This is how she knows they are gaining some command of Japanese; they are actually using it contextually. Strong (2002, p. 4) notes that "new vocabulary and concepts are disconnected from experience and prior knowledge" of the learner.

This strategy should be transferred to all other subjects and classes. We all find it enormously difficult to read and interact with words that we cannot say. In short, a math teacher should teach math as a language and might do well to try these tactics:

All students repeat the word aloud: *"Okay, kids, let's all say this one loudly, clearly: polynomial. Again, with real feeling. Everybody, say it again."*

Invite one student to define the term in front of the class while classmates in pairs are asked to paraphrase the definition without using one word that the designated student used in his or her definition. *"You all have two minutes to make this translation. You may use images, examples, whatever it takes, but not one word our designated definer used. Go."*

Call upon the pairs to present their definition with an emphasis on active listening: *"If a pair has a paraphrase that comes close to yours, raise your hands so that we can see how we're all doing on this one."*

Use these paraphrasing sessions as a means to assess the accuracy of student perceptions of the definition.

We need to ask students to demonstrate their understanding through translation of terms into their own vernacular. A demonstration can take the form of an analogy, an application, an example, an illustration, or a conversation. This method contrasts with the instructional tendency to define a term in front of the class, jot down that definition, have them copy it, and test them on their ability to memorize the definition. Focused classroom conversation is an anchor activity in any foreign language class. The value of this strategy is obvious when students begin to discuss these specialized terms with each other. They are gaining increasing comfort and confidence with the very concepts requisite for engaging in the curriculum. Conversation in the classroom is valuable because students learn to work together to solve problems using the subject area language as they do so. This simulates what students do in foreign language classes as well.

Personal Power Words

> "I admit painfully that for the past thirty years, I have worked on the assumption that the kids I teach walk into our high school with a certain level of language proficiency and that there is nothing I can do about it," said Mr. Davidson, a seasoned science teacher. "Some kids could write and speak well for themselves. Some kids just didn't have it. Some kids could read the science text, and some kids couldn't, so they didn't. There was nothing I could do to help, or so I thought."

Mr. Davidson is a changed man—and an improved teacher—because he heeded the advice of his colleagues and began generating a highly visible word bank for each unit of study. These words are not high-frequency words commonly seen in text. They are not highly specialized terms representing a key subject matter concept. Rather, these words are simply vivid, precise, engaging words that enhance and give power to thinking in print and in speech. In his chemistry class, his students' lab reports were boring, flat, and imprecise, even though they employed technically complete sentences: "It went down the test tube." "This experiment was interesting." The writing lacked adjectives, was filled with passive verbs, and contained virtually no adverbs. The labs begged for revision. In short, Mr. Davidson stepped up his role as a science teacher to that of a science teacher who gives his students a critical tool for better science: better words.

Mr. Davidson now requires his students to employ at least five of these words or to supply alternatives that they add to the word bank for every lab. What is more impressive is that the students turn in their first draft with the revisions showing. He not only teaches science; he teaches revision as well.

Rachel, a sophomore, describes her experiment in chemistry with words like *constricted*, *diminished*, *restricted*, *expanded*, *trickled*, or *oozed*. These are words generated by the class and Mr. Davidson on a prominent word wall. Needless to say, Rachel's lab reports have improved. She and her classmates now re-read the assignment, sometimes catch an editing problem, and always improve the quality of their work. This result shows that students' work improves if a teacher gives them words generously and requires them to actually use them actively. Our Japanese teacher, Ms.

Momiji, like every language teacher, gives students words to use and expects them to use them. All teachers should take a cue from the language teachers who lavish students with words, expecting students not only to hear them, but also to speak them.

We should be pumping our students full of words. Although teachers engage in the well established practice of giving out vocabulary lists of words developed by English teachers for students to look up and define and use in a sentence, these words are often de-contextualized or simply lifted from ongoing literature studies. What is rare is for the words to actually be used, especially in a natural context, outside of a discussion about a particular work of literature. Providing a list of enriched words that make sense for application in any given unit, posting them with the highest visibility, and then requiring their usage in assignments are key to improving student success across the curriculum. There is a natural context to expanded vocabulary, and students who employ these words in one context will find themselves using this vocabulary in subjects outside of English class.

Students see immediate results when teachers feed them words generously. If a fourth grader is studying how seeds grow into plants, the term *photosynthesis* has special meaning. Although teachers need to focus on specialized terms, the revision strategy suggested here is about giving Abdul the tools to revise his work while increasing his understanding. To replace a word is not simply to ornament a sentence; it injects power and life into it. A command of words breeds confidence. Students know the difference between the pretentious use of words and the precise use of words.

When high school students cram for the SAT test and start memorizing laundry lists of vocabulary words, it is disconcerting for them and for their teachers. The words are lost within a very few weeks. While waiters can keep a long list of today's specials in their heads, they will not retain that list. Why should they? They're done with that information. "List learning" is temporary. We are striving for durable learning, where what is learned stays learned and is used. The deployment of vocabulary words assists students. I recommend that teachers post and develop word banks for each subject. There may be particular adjectives and verbs that increase the level of performance of each learner.

Consider the seventh graders who are creating personal responses to a work of literature. They can present their points of view using the language that they have at their fingertips. Children are not born with these vocabulary lists. We can improve the performance of all of our students by handing them words and showing them how to revise their current work. Johnny needs a generous teacher. So Mr. Travis, his social studies teacher, says, "Okay, students, tonight when you write your letter to Thomas Jefferson, please use five adjectives from our class collaborative word bank and five verbs, or add new ones that you find. Just be sure to add them to our word wall."

Interactive Thesaurus

A particularly powerful digital application that can assist students in cultivating a love of words is Visual Thesaurus, developed by Think Map. Not only can a student have words literally explode into a web of possible synonyms—these very words are pronounced so the user can hear them, as indicated in the small speaker sign next to the word in the center of Figure 2.3. Definitions and clarification of the part of speech are indicated

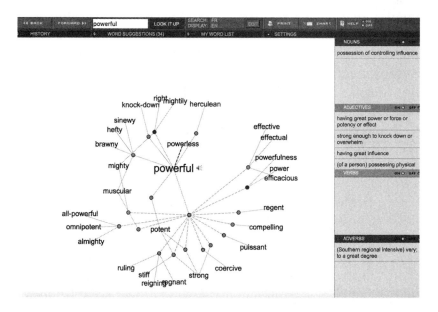

FIGURE 2.3 Dynamic development of personal power words using Visual Thesaurus.com

on the side bar coupled with additional features to translate the words into other languages.

The visual display of moving words can stimulate the interest of learners who often find vocabulary building as dull. What is more, as with any quality educational app there is depth to the functions. Visual Thesaurus supports "Vocab-grabber," which sorts words from any text that is copied into subject area specialization. This latter capability supports the previously identified specialized terminology word types.

Summary

Ask any teacher who has scored the written essays on the Advanced Placement examinations about the importance of vocabulary. Two student essays that fundamentally state the exact same premise, with the exact same details and with accurate language mechanics and grammar are scored differently on the basis of the quality of the diction. If one student provides a more lucid and insightful view because of the words selected for the essay, then he or she should be rewarded. One of the most effective ways to improve scoring performance is the use of increased and expansive vocabulary. Mastery of vocabulary not only produces immediate results in writing, but also significantly affects reading. We can read the words we understand, and we understand the words we use effectively. By developing and using a powerful descriptive vocabulary, a reader will know these words when he or she encounters them in any context.

In order to promote language expansion, a teacher can design classroom experiences that enable learners to develop three distinctive types of vocabulary:

◆ **High-frequency words** are taught across all subjects. The key is that teachers request that students translate the words into their own vernacular on all assignments. I recommend that several workbook lines be left open for students to translate the directions. A list of translations can be posted in any class with student paraphrases of high-frequency words.

◆ **Specialized terminology** is best taught in the course of introducing content and key concepts. To assess whether students understand the meaning of these terms, teachers can require students to demonstrate their understanding rather than simply to recopy a definition out of a textbook. Students should be asked to demonstrate the meaning of the word through an analogy or a real-world application.

◆ **Personal power words** are best taught through a specific unit of study. For example, adjectives may be listed in a unit on Life in the Desert that will be helpful in descriptions: arid, dry, sweeping, intense, shifting.

Table 2.1 provides examples of high-frequency words, specialized terminology, and personal power words from three different classrooms.

Our students face increasing language challenges as they enter the upper elementary grades and move on into secondary school. Their teachers make more assumptions about what

TABLE 2.1 Curriculum examples using the three word types

High Frequency Words	Specialized Terminology	Personal Power Words
Third Grade Unit: *Life Under the Sea*		
Examine	Plankton	Fluid
Select	Coral	Turbulent
Discuss	Reef	Intricate
Identify	Bay	Placid
Seventh Grade Unit: *World War II*		
Infer	Fascism	Formidable
Interpret	Truce	Contentious
Posit	Platoon	Preventable
Analyze	Totalitarian	Strategic
Eleventh Grade Unit: *Hamlet*		
Extrapolate	Archetype	Quixotic
Dissuade	Monologue	Subversive
Refute	Prologue	Charismatic
Concede	Irony	Querulous

they comprehend, even as the language becomes more abstract. Furthermore, given the surge in the number of students, teachers in middle and high schools rely on more independent reading from each learner. And, on top of all of this, explicit instruction in reading diminishes unless the student receives special education services. Because of these factors, many of our students are left behind, unable to master the increasing difficulty of the subject matter in the higher grade levels.

By engaging students in three separately developed forms of vocabulary building, teachers see how these forms cross disciplines. Imagine if all of Johnny's, Rachel's, Abdul's, and Maria's teachers helped them become stronger masters of the English language.

Teachers from every discipline can contribute to student success by separating vocabulary into three distinctive types with distinctive instructional approaches in order to increase student literacy.

3

Activating Notemaking

Extraction, Reaction, and Sketchnoting

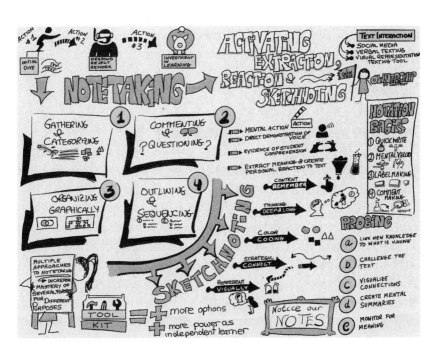

Illustration by Silvia Tolisano

Taking notice of what matters most is at the heart of critical thought. Notetaking should be packed with mental action: it involves creative engagement. Notetaking is a direct demonstration of voice. Interactive notetaking provides revealing evidence of authentic student comprehension from both written, aural, and multimedia sources. Interactive notetaking replaces the frequent reliance for evaluation of comprehension on *simulated* reading evidence, such as fill-in-the-blank sheets or predetermined multiple-choice examinations. Interactive notetaking asks Rachel to extract meaning from written, aural, visual and media sources and to create her personal and selective reaction.

In the past if we had asked teachers which fundamental skills are lacking in their learners, they might have replied that their students display weak comprehension and are passive responders. Passive students are bred when they are continually asked to play "fetch" in class. Fetch occurs when a teacher asks a restrictive question that seeks one answer. The student then goes out to fetch that prize. The knowledge is not the student's. I believe that the use of social media tools, verbal texting, and visual representation texting tools can serve as a useful basis for increasing "text interaction" in classical reading and listening.

Texting as a Basis for Active Notetaking

The surge of texting has forced the issue of quick summation and abbreviation to a new foundation for refining interactive notemaking. Adults and young people who use personal devices and smart phones rely on the ability to quickly communicate with others through efficient summary language replete with clever abbreviations (LOL, BTW) and emoticons. It is an integrated part of daily communication, and we should not run from it in our classroom world. In the traditional approach to notetaking, shorthand was always a central skill set. In truth, basic texting is shorthand, and there should be no confusion as to the difference between sending a message about meeting someone for coffee and notetaking regarding the meaning of a novel. The question for our consideration is how to develop meaningful content for learning using many of the new tools available given digital tools and social media.

Twitter has the potential to raise the bar with the insistent need to get to the central idea in 140 characters. One of the most engaging Twitter sites I like to share is Real Time World War II, developed by Oxford University history graduate, Alwyn Collison, who posts daily images and events AS IF he were alive during World War II from a wide range of perspectives, whether a soldier or a citizen. What we should attend to for our purposes is his ability to capture the key idea in the entries seen in Figure 3.1.

Collison shows us how to capture the main idea in the nutshell called Twitter. Might we consider asking our students to similarly make notations using a twitter style to raise key questions or to pose essential elements for communication? An

FIGURE 3.1 Real Time World War II on Twitter developed by Alwyn Collison engages viewers with primary source photos and infographics coupled with engaging thumbnail accounts

English lit teacher in Athens, Georgia, asked her students to select a character from the Canterbury Tales and to interact on the class hashtag. Fifth graders in Jacksonville, Florida, make entries on the class Twitter account regarding a photo of animal bones that they have located on the grounds of the school in order to figure out the species. They send their tweets to veterinarians, zoology professors, and researchers who all converge on a common feed. With the fifth graders, the group reaches consensus that it an opossum. The point here is that the ability to DISTILL words and get at what is noteworthy is certainly a notetaking skill, but when it is coupled with social outreach and connection the power is amplified.

I find it odd how frequently the ability to copy is mistaken for notetaking. Copying is copying. If a teacher requests that students copy a phrase from the *Gettysburg Address*, then the task is clear. But frequently we ask students to take notes from the notes that the teacher put on the blackboard. What we are assessing here is the students' ability to copy the teacher's ability to take notes. There is little or no interaction—just words. Neon highlighting pens have dramatically produced lime, fuchsia, lemon, and tangerine, glowingly lit student workbooks, articles, and assignments. These pens generate the perception that underlining is notetaking. Underlining is underlining. How do we know when students are reading with meaning? Certainly not by just looking at them. Consider this scenario of a study hall where students are supposed to be reading.

> Faking reading during study hall has become a well-developed art form at James High. With years of practice under their belts, the juniors and seniors in fourth period study hall scrunch their eyebrows and burrow deeply into their texts as the monitor, Mr. Adams, meanders through the round tables in the corner of the school library. As he passes, his trail can be followed by watching the flow of heads lifting slightly from the books, smiles glancing across tables, until prior activity is resumed. Mr. Adams has taken his requisite constitutional stroll and will return to marking papers in the corner.

Study hall is a way to lessen the length of a school day by 45 minutes by doing on school time that which should be done off of school time. More telling, however, is that there was mutual collusion on the reading question. In order to know if the James High students were actually interacting with their text, as opposed to simply looking at marks on a page, there is a need for evidence. The evidence is not only for their teachers, but also, first and foremost, for the students. Looking at a student looking at a page has never served as sufficient evidence of reading.

Creative notetaking requires *extraction* and *reaction*. The students' ability to extract and explain core ideas, concepts, and factual details is revealed in their notes. The students' ability to sort and classify these extractions is central to their comprehension of the text's meaning. Their competence at commenting and responding to the notes is a sign of interaction and ownership of the material.

My work on Curriculum Mapping suggests that teachers in school settings struggle with when to introduce or who should introduce notetaking. No one is to blame; we simply did not have the means in the past to provide sufficient real-time data to find out precisely the specific way notetaking is introduced and developed. Clearly it is a K–12 skill that evolves developmentally over time. There are multiple approaches to notetaking, and students need to increase their mastery of several formats for different purposes.

This chapter identifies central problems in current classroom practice regarding notetaking, defines four distinct forms for notetaking, and develops a set of requisite baseline notetaking competencies written in student-friendly language.

Taking Notice of Notetaking Problems

Here are some of the problems: (1) Teachers within a building and between buildings define notetaking differently. (2) They have the vague expectation that students should come into their classes with this skill already formed. (3) Teachers deal with notetaking too broadly, as opposed to more formally with four specific notetaking genres. (4) The notes themselves are often missed as critical assessment data to determine whether students are truly interacting with the text.

A review of numerous notetaking approaches makes clear that many of them are taught as separate skills with little apparent link to content. Some school programs have one teacher introduce a notetaking approach, but there is little, if any, formal assessment of its integration in all classes. Furthermore, some notetaking programs suggest that there is only one method for notetaking, thus limiting the menu of options to assist a range of learners. In contrast, students should leave school equipped with a range of specific notetaking and notemaking strategies (Strong, 2002). Notetaking requires different types of language proficiencies. There are four fundamental sources for notes:

♦ Written text, aural (speaking or sounds)
♦ Visual sources (graphic images, paintings, charts)
♦ Visual with aural sources (television, film, interactive websites)
♦ Live performances (dance, music, sports)

Not all students have equal strengths in dealing with each of these sources. Not all teachers have equal strengths in employing these sources in their teaching. In truth, some teachers and students are easier to listen to than others. Some books, films, and images are more compelling than others for specific learners. A sporting event might be confusing rather than engaging if a student doesn't know the rules of the game. In short, learners need assistance in red-flagging those sources that might prove challenging and where additional support is needed. Certainly our learners need to practice using various notetaking forms in response to various source materials.

Four Notetaking Forms
My review of curriculum reveals four types of notetaking, which can be described using action verbs. Each of the forms is identified with verbal protocols to indicate the active nature of the

notetaking task. Different types of classroom tasks match different types of notetaking formats. All notetaking promotes actions that the learners take. Most students have a passive picture of notetaking in their minds that we need to counteract with a vigorous counterview of notetaking. Notetaking must become creative. The four forms for CREATING notes are:

♦ Gathering and Categorizing
♦ Commenting and Questioning
♦ Organizing and Connecting
♦ Outlining and Sequencing Sets

In the first edition of this book I had identified the third form as "organizing graphically," but have seen over the past decade a decided shift into using visual tools and visible thinking in all forms. Thus, prior to diving into each of the notetaking forms, we will consider the notion of sketchnoting as a central option and necessary skill set for our learners.

Sketchnoting for Each of the Four Forms

In the spirit of employing modern tools and approaches, the emergence of readily available and easy to use digital applications allow for extraction and reaction to be displayed using Sketchnoting formats. A leader in this burgeoning field is Silvia Tolisano, who has created a sketchnote about sketchnoting in Figure 3.2.

In a recent blog post, Silvia reflects on her own journey of moving from traditional notes in a notebook to visual sketchnoting using digital tools such as *Paper 53*:

I have noticed the following as part of the process of sketchnoting as note taking:

♦ doodling/sketching my notes makes me remember the content better and longer
♦ the act of 'coloring' (filling in block letters or objects) gives me time to think deeper and longer about the meaning.

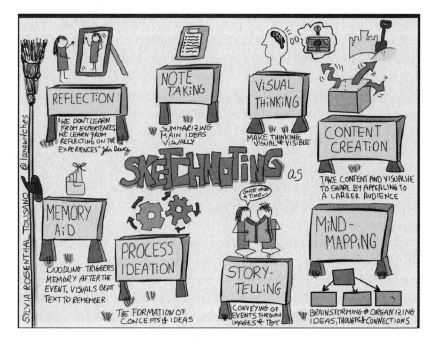

FIGURE 3.2 Silvia Tolisano provides an image of moving from traditional notes using sketchnoting techniques

- ◆ choosing colors adds another dimension of organization, hierarchy and connectivity between concepts and ideas.
- ◆ the act of thinking about the visual representation of a point or concept adds depth to understanding that point or concept.
- ◆ choosing strategic arrows and connectors help make sense of an overall message and 'how is this related to a bigger picture?'

(Tolisano, 2015)

Giving our reflections form is really what writing notes has been about on the most fundamental level; the form itself has been words. With sketchnoting we are combining words with images and graphic relationships. In her blog post for KQED in San Francisco, *Making Learning Visible: Doodling Makes Memories Stick*, Katrina Schwartz (2015) notes:

While doodling has often been seen as frivolous at best and distracting at worst, the idea of sketchnoting has grounding in neuroscience research about how to improve memory. When ideas and related concepts can be encapsulated in an image, the brain remembers the information associated with that image.

Schwartz (2015) cites the work of Professor William Klemm from Texas A&M University, who has coined the phrase "story chains" as a visual method for student to connect thoughts with a string of images and words. These story chains are in essence sketchnoting and can powerfully assist memory.

Finding what is noteworthy is like mining. This is the extraction component of the work involved in notetaking. When searching for a pivotal idea or for a specific detail, the student burrows into the text and pulls out the "note." Johnny takes the note out of the text, whether it is written, visual, or aural. The response to the note, the comment, is Johnny's reaction. When a student interacts with the noteworthy notion by jotting a response, it becomes his or her own. Thus, interactive notetaking provides clear and revealing evidence of the student's genuine understanding in the act of reading, viewing, and/or listening.

Each of the four types is distinctive in both task and response. There is no one preferred notetaking approach; instead, I believe that if Maria has all four types securely in her toolkit, she has more options and more power as an independent learner.

Creating Notes Through *Gathering* and *Categorizing*

This form of notetaking develops the student's ability to rake in information from a range of sources, sift through the details and main ideas, and group and regroup findings into categories. A key aspect of gathering is the specific driving question that focuses the gathering. I believe that using essential questions or guiding questions is enormously helpful. The question serves as a kind of "mental velcro" to which information will "stick."

For example, when Abdul is asked to search generic informa-tion in his seventh grade unit on Ancient China, the subject is so vast that he has trouble finding salient information. If, in contrast, he has a question to guide his search—e.g., What have been major contributions of the Ancient Chinese to civilization?—and if the teacher asks him to extract all of the material in his textbook or from the Internet that sticks to the question like Velcro, then he has a mission for his search. Now he has a stack of either physical or virtual notecards on the historical contributions from China. He now needs to make meaning, to make sense, of the cards. If he can sort through them and put them together in piles by common factors that he develops, and if he can label those factors, then that information and his schema make them his knowledge. A student might use a tool like Quizlet, which allows the student to create a virtual stack of flashcards with answers that can be tested via games (see Figure 3.3).

FIGURE 3.3 Quizlet.com provides students with interactive information and vocabulary building tools

This interactive notetaking approach commences in preschool or kindergarten when youngsters collect important objects, list important ideas, and pull out important details in stories. Determining the difference between what is important and what is not important can even be its own category. As a start, I recommend that learners identify concrete categories as they hunt through source material. When a teacher reads a story out loud, students can make notes periodically in a formal fashion with pictures, icons, or simple words. They can then cluster these notes into groups and see how they might be presented. An analogy to making a scrapbook is useful here, for the same questions apply: What do we save and why? How do we organize what we save? Digital tools can assist in posting the work, such as the impressive Kindgarten Padlet from Sharon Davison's class at Allen Brook School in Williston, Vermont (see Figure 3.4).

In the third through fifth grades, I recommend that students use jumbo notecards upon which they enter their findings and

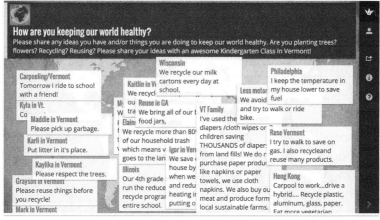

FIGURE 3.4 Ms. Davison's Padlet for her kindergarten class

set up categories. I prefer index cards to notebook paper because students can shuffle the cards around and write on the back of them. For example, Ms. Adams may ask her students to study life in the desert, turning them loose with books, videos, and the Internet to collect data. On each card, students make entries with a bibliographical reference and by color.

For example, Maria, an eight-year-old student, culls some information from a book titled *Animals of the Desert*. Because this book is on the class book list as #1, any entry from that book is simply registered with a #1 at the top right hand corner. Maria continues to collect twelve cards from three sources. She places the cards on the table and, at her teacher's request, starts to look at all of the different ways she might categorize her findings. She moves the cards around the table as manipulatives. Maria has four possible groups: (a) animals that live underground; (b) animals that live above ground; (c) animals my mother would let me keep; (d) animals that can live only in the desert. Obviously, Maria has wrestled with her notes. She knows them in part because she worked with them on the tabletop.

Maria shares her categories and her notes with two other children, Abdul and Johnny. They devise somewhat different groups, but in class discussion they discover that their notes show many commonalities. These students have interacted with the notes, the labels, and each others' categories, reflecting multiple levels of engagement. These categories help to lead us to that most difficult concept: finding the main idea.

Having perused many K–12 curriculum maps, I am always amazed to find how often one of the goals at every grade level is the skill of *finding the main idea*. I think that Ms. Adams and her upper elementary colleagues have reached a critical point when their students can look for and begin to differentiate between what is main and what is trivial, between what makes a viable category and what does not hold up under scrutiny. Students need practice making categories. It is a central skill that is necessary for one to become a logical and analytical thinker.

Gathering and categorizing continue to evolve into more complex forms as students move into middle and high school. Whether pursuing information in the investigation of a research question or doing an initial reading exploration to frame such a question, the secondary student should feel comfortable and confident in collecting a wide range of information. His ability to group and regroup and reorder and rethink the note entries is central to bona fide research. Immersion in the material must go beyond copying.

I believe that this ability is critical to the study skills of our learners. A striking passivity characterizes research projects when there is no real search. To search again, to *research*, suggests that the scholar must revisit the data and sift through it actively, organizing and reorganizing. The secondary student, in the same spirit as the elementary student, can categorize material on cards, on a desk, or on a computer with a simple program like *Inspiration*. The manipulation of the data and the framing of headings as either concepts or questions propel students into interaction.

Research should not be taught; it is research and development (R&D) that should be taught. The development of categories and the mental analysis that it represents are at the heart of authentic and active intellectual pursuits. To research is to search again. It is through making labels and developing our own schemes that we provide meaning to our first searches.

Creating Notes Through *Commenting* and *Questioning*

When I was a doctoral student at Teachers College, Columbia University, New York City, in the late 1970s, I had a seminar with Professor Phil Phenix on "Educational Classics of the West." For the course we were to thoroughly read great books written by great Western thinkers. In order to raise the quality and nature of our engagement, Dr. Phenix asked us to buy paperback copies and to write in the margins. We were not simply to underscore key points, but rather to *grill the author*. This was not to be a pseudointellectual barbeque, but rather an opportunity to enter into an imaginary argument with the likes of Rousseau, St. Augustine, Bertrand Russell, Sir Alfred North Whitehead, Immanuel Kant, and John Dewey. Wisely, our professor wanted us to comment on and probe into the ideas of some remarkable minds. In the course of our imaginary interactions, we took ownership of the premises and tenets, manipulated them like mental clay, and absorbed them or rejected them as critical thinkers. Professor Phenix knew the value of note-sparring.

I see a counterpart to this graduate school example in primary classrooms when teachers ask their students to use "Post-Its." A child reads a story like *Sylvester and the Pebble* and is asked to write questions for Sylvester and "post" them right on the page. "Coach Sylvester," the second grade teacher says, "Help him get out of this tough situation." The seven-year-old students in this class are interacting in a way that is vital and immediate. There is a purpose to their reading. They must take in Sylvester's dilemma and respond. Their notes are active as they create comments.

Post-Its as Physicalized Interactions

The invention of the post-it was a brilliant invention born from a mistake. In 1968 Spencer Silver, an inventor at the 3M laboratories, was attempting to create an exceptionally strong adhesive. What he actually developed stuck to objects, but could be lifted off with ease. No one could figure out what do with this new adhesive. It wasn't until six years later when a colleague, Arthur Fry, determined that he could use the invention to hold his bookmarks to his hymnbook, which were perpetually falling off (Donnelly, 2012).

When post-its found their way into classroom life, teachers had a new way to show that students were literally *on the page*. The physical demonstration of notetaking was amplified so that students would sit at their desks with textbooks filled with a rainbow pallet of colorful post-its (often neon no less).

We now have *electronic post-its or marginal comment notes* that not only work effectively at any level of education, but also can be used in areas that are not usually targeted for such interactions. Certainly this practice is used widely in literature, with students making comments about characters in a story, but interactions and comments should occur consistently in all subjects. For example, math teachers can assign students a post-it task to raise questions and make observations in their math textbooks regarding a new skill or concept being addressed: "For tonight's homework, post your questions and comments about the trickiest steps when dividing mixed fractions. We'll see if you have some shared observations tomorrow." The next day students come into class, sit in groups, and compare their interactions with the text. The post-it can be from a digital tool or a paper post-it, but key is that the interaction reflects learner ownership of the comment.

Social studies teachers can ask students to grill Thomas Jefferson about the *Declaration of Independence:* "Ask him tough questions. Ask him questions not only about the contradictions between his lifestyle and his words, but also about any specific wording choices." The idea is to *probe*. Questioning is a means through which students can attain comprehension. This probing creates opportunities for students to link new knowledge to what is known, to challenge the texts, to visualize connections, to create mental summaries, and to monitor for meaning. To investigate and burrow into the ideas presented in Jefferson's writing is the essence of critical thought. Effective notetaking documents the student's personal observations. So much in social studies is about POV, the point of view given by a writer at any age; thus, there is a multitude of opportunities for an elementary school teacher to lead students to comment and question. The root word for *story* is embedded in the word *history*. Students can be assigned to make Post-It comments throughout a book in response to the question, "Who is telling the story?" Ask them questions that reveal their point of view, their bias, their perspective.

There are obvious opportunities for probing in science, yet often students take very superficial notes that do not lead to a deeper level of inquiry. Ironically, science classes, which are based on investigation, often employ routinized notes, the copied note. If a biology teacher hands Rachel a set of his personal science notes for her to keep, then what is actually being assessed is whether or not she will lose them. Students need to develop both the ability to extract pertinent data and retain specific facts (which the biology teacher did for Rachel) and to form links between these facts as evidence in personal comments.

Comments in science can emphasize probing and promote finding analogies. Assignments can suggest opportunities for students to find these links.

I recently heard an AP Chemistry teachers tell her students, "Tonight, as you read through the text on the periodic chart of the elements, make your notes in the form of analogies using family. How is calcium like the brother to iron? You can create a godfather relationship or clan. But show relationships in your comments, and construct questions that you might ask this 'cast of characters.'" The proof is in the pudding. Ask these chemistry students to describe the relationship between the elements on the chart two months after the assignment, and compare their understanding to that of the students who merely copied the material. Extraction and reaction are at the core of direct engagement with the text.

Textbooks themselves are highly cued so that the reader is directed to important and supportive information through titles, headings, subheadings, chapter summaries, chapter questions, charts, graphs, and pictures. Students can be instructed to reflect these cues directly in their notes if it is helpful. In a sense, they can use them as milestones that can link their personal notations with the book that they are "touring."

A simple and powerful commenting and probing format is the split page. Students divide a piece of paper in half: on one side, they place the extracted key ideas; on the opposite side, they place their comments and reactions. This can be done in a fourth grade class reading about colonial America, where students are asked to find key events in each colony while making corresponding observations or questions that they might ask the targeted colonial group. The split page can be used at any level. It is a clear and simple way to have students see that one side of the page contains the extractions and that the other side contains their personal reactions through comments and questions. We need students to develop competencies in both columns.

An easily accessible approach to group interaction is through a Google doc, where designated learners can interact over shared text or images with their comments and immediate chat. I recommend that teachers keep copies of these comments and interactions and use them as text with their learners at the end of a unit of study to reflect on how individual thinking and collaborative interactions have developed through the course of the unit.

Creating Notes by *Organizing and Connecting*

By reshaping text ideas either from writing or listening and placing them into a visual mode, students are owning material. The effectiveness of visual charting is well documented in business and educational circles. Drawing linked shapes and connective lines creates analogous mirrors of cognitive understandings. Graphic organizers for the learner should be personal and act as a kind of conceptual real estate. The student is saying, "This is how I have staked out my ideas and organized them. This is what it looks like." Graphic organizers are a particularly striking way to evoke relationships and systems. English teachers frequently ask students to show the plot structure of a novel graphically. Mr. Jones asks his ninth graders who are reading Harper Lee's *To Kill a Mockingbird* to graphically represent the relationship between all of the major characters in that southern town that remarkable summer. This graphic representation presents evidence of how Abdul sees Atticus linked to Scout and to Boo Radley and to the town itself. Mr. Jones can now have confidence that when Abdul writes his observations about the text, they will be clearer to him because of this notetaking organizer. Math teachers could do the same with an algorithm, or science teachers by showing progressive views of the solar system through the eyes of various astronomers in history.

Depictions of webs are used frequently to represent possible clusters of common factors and put them in a visual display. The point is that we need to break out of the stagnant way we ask students to make sense out of their work. If we ask for pedestrian schemes, we will get them. Graphic organizers can be stale, too, but they have the potential for invigorating investigations.

Graphic organizers identify relationships because they can be displayed in visual form. The term *flow chart* reflects the fluid nature of systemic components. Although graphic organizers can go awry when applied without sufficient regard to the kind of material to be reformulated, what is important is that students identify the relationship between the graphic shapes themselves. It is easy for a learner to simply put something in a flow-chart box as a kind of "filler."

Imagine how useful it would be for a high school sophomore studying world history to be asked midyear to reflect on the major historical eras, themes, and key events and to create a graphic organizer showing their relationship. This kind of interaction is highly conceptual and creative. Graphic organizers make excellent prewriting activities.

David Hyerle, a leading educator in assisting students in creating graphic displays, developed a set of templates that help students see the possibilities *of translating* textual forms into visual ones; e.g., a Venn diagram reflects the overlap and differences between a set of concepts. It is of real value for students to look at a form and orally describe what they believe the "graphic form" suggests as a concept by its shape. In this way Johnny can select a form that matches his idea rather than forcing his ideas into an assigned graphic form. "Thinking Maps offers a language that combines symbols: All other symbolic and pictorial representations may be used within each map" (Hyerle and Alper, 2011, p. 3).

Digital graphic organizing tools have increased the motivation to graphically represent meaning—not only is it easier, but also it is more fun for learners. Tools such as Mindmeister and Bubbl.us (Figure 3.5) make it easy for students to select a tool that matches a purpose. There are also dynamic collaborative graphic organizers such as Lucid Chart (Figure 3.6) or ImindMap that allow a group to collectively and simultaneously plan and work virtually through their own original organizers as in the example in Figure 3.6 between a group of teachers and administrators.

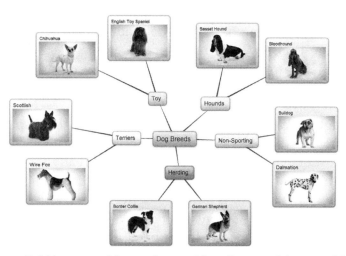

FIGURE 3.5 Bubble.us provides students with a direct tool for visual learning and representation

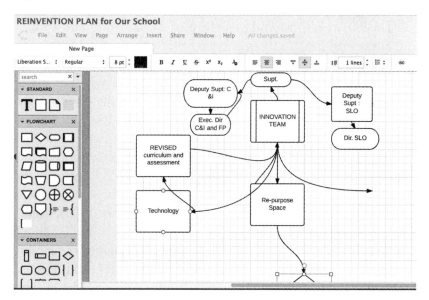

FIGURE 3.6 Lucid Chart allows users to share commonly made graphic organizers for group work

Creating Notes by *Outlining* and *Sequencing* Sets

"I think it makes sense that whoever invented outlining chose the Roman numerals, because the Romans were into such a power trip," said Isaac, a sixth grader from a New York City middle school where I was working. Isaac had a point. There is a tremendous emphasis on order and sequence in outlining, and there is also a wide range of situations where the highly sequential nature of the outlining is both practical and useful in organizing ideas. The problem for our students is the overemphasis on *the numerals themselves*. The key concept to be taught in outlining is *larger to smaller*. When Isaac successfully figures out the relationship between broader concepts and the details that can support them, he is ready for structuring the outlining scaffold. He can add the Roman numerals themselves almost as an afterthought. I have heard students complain, "I get so confused about whether to have a small 'a' or a capital 'A' or whether I need parentheses or not that I miss the whole point." The point of the outlining approach is to provide students with a direct form of organizing sets of ideas in a natural sequence.

The linear nature and structure of Roman numeral outlining are useful for tightly sequenced plotting. Students often get confused by the top-down nature of outlining. A more useful description comes from a middle school teacher who compares outlining to "laying train tracks." Each track depends on the next; there has to be a natural sequence; and there has to be latticework to support each track. Each track is analogous to a central concept and can be placed on the route only when there are sufficient details to support it. The rails are the focus of the work and give the direction, the plot of the journey. If a track does not maintain and forge ahead within the focus (the rails), then it is superfluous to the direction of the work. In short, students need to sift through their investigations to determine what is relevant to their topic and what should not be laid down as tracks. This more lateral view is more understandable than the top-down view.

We often pay too much attention to the numerals themselves. The youngest children in K–2 begin by using attribute blocks to convey the concept of *larger to smaller*. The concept of a broad idea or observation supported by smaller details is very hard to teach in the abstract. I recommend that younger learners compile sets of larger to smaller objects on tables and examine each other's sequences. For example, one can use a picture of a garden with pictures of different flowers supporting it. Eventually, as students move into the upper elementary grades, they can move to textual phrases but still lay them out on a table, e.g., with sentence strips. A sentence such as "Rivers have played a central role in early civilizations" can be supported with pictures and phrases from the Nile River, Yangtze River, or the Tigris and Euphrates Rivers as elements supporting the topic sentence.

In one high school I saw an extremely effective use of cafeteria tables to help freshmen lay out their outlines. The subject was a study of the Medieval Period, and each student had collected many index cards with extractions on key points regarding the way people lived on feudal estates. The teacher asked them to put them in sets and label them with a common factor on the top. A rubber band was put around each set. She then asked the students to identify possible ways to sequence those labels, and they literally had to lay them out (like train tracks) on the cafeteria tables. When this was accomplished, the teacher had them open the banded sets and lay them under each topic. She then told them to use a Roman numeral outline system to collect the sequence of sets of topic cards and the supporting detail cards. The students got it. They understood for the first time that outlining is a superb organizer.

Although this note cards and labeling exercise seems like a slow approach, I do believe that it accentuates the LOGIC behind outlining in a way that simply jumping into the built-in tools available on Microsoft Word or Pages provides. For example when using Microsoft word, Issac selects Outline from the View tab on the tool bar. He then can click the Outline View button from the view buttons in the lower left corner of the document window, and then his document will be shown as if it were an outline. It can be expanded or collapsed by double clicking on the plus symbols next to the major headings. The outline is based upon the styles and indents that he used in his document. To reiterate, our learners clearly need to "get" why the format matters rather than simply jump to the tools.

Student-Friendly Notation Basics

When students have a clear knowledge of the four basic types of notetaking, teachers can assist them to develop expertise in each type. An aid to the acquisition of this expertise is the use of notation basics. Students benefit from clear, user-friendly terms that describe the four basic skills they need to effectively use the four basic types of notetaking from any source material. All teachers in a building might use these basics to communicate in a fun and clear way.

Quick-Write

The ability to write quickly is often overlooked in student notetaking preparation. In using traditional pen and pencil formats, too many learners copy the entire page into their notebooks, whereas others are clueless about which important phrases are the ones to select. In the lower grades students can learn how to use images and icons in an effective manner. By upper elementary school, students should practice eliminating words for notes. They should begin to recognize which words should be included and which should be left out when listening to a teacher's presentation. Middle and high school students can actually have timed practice at notetaking because they will have to learn to budget their notetaking energies effectively. After doing this, students can exchange notes to see what other people find important and to reinforce learning.

Building on the ability of many of our students to TEXT with great rapidity is an opener to engaging them in TEXTING their curricular notations. In short, they CAN write quickly but tend to think of texting as a personal family or friend interaction. What if we applied this same skill set to learning experiences in school or virtually? Consider the example from San Francisco, where students are using Twitter to interact with a lesson guided by their teacher:

www.resetsanfrancisco.org/education/crowdsourcing-classroom-education-2-0/

Mental Velcro

Students need to know the "sticking point" when they engage in reading, listening, and viewing. They need to ask, "What am I looking for? What do I need to extract?" These essential questions serve as a kind of mental velcro so that students can extract everything that sticks to the *essential question* when they read a chapter. When one primary grade teacher reads aloud from Lobel's *Frog and Toad*, she has one child wear a "velcro jacket" with the question: "What makes a good friend?" When students finish listening to the book, they write down phrases and ideas from the story and literally stick them on the jacket. When another teacher of fourth graders asks students to read about different types of rocks and minerals, she begins the lesson with the essential question: "What stories about the earth can we find in examining a rock?" The students read the chapter and note all of the points in the chapter that stick to the question. A high school student might read about World War II and, instead of trying to gather information randomly, search for all pertinent information that sticks to the question, "Was World War II inevitable?"

Label-Making and Digital Tagging

After students compile notes and comments from an investigation using an essential question, they can make different groupings and literal piles of these notes. Critical is that the students create a label that designates a common factor. For instance, the notes from the fourth graders mentioned above might contain common information about where the rocks come from or they might show different uses for the rocks and minerals. Students need to acquire the basic ability to find a word or two that suggests the common factor. It is the creating of the label that reflects text-interaction.

A great and current example of category and label making is in the tagging of digital tools in order to make navigation on our devises easier. In my definition of capacities necessary for digital literacy (Jacobs, 2014, p. 7), supporting students in selecting, tagging, and curating digital tools is central to cultivating digitally literate learners in that they are slowing down to make judgments about the quality of an application and then owning it through the labeling process. Simply looking at one's smart phone or tablet it is clear that we choose those apps, cluster them, and then label that group in order to navigate through the myriad of apps and tools that are possible. For example, Figure 3.7 reflects

FIGURE 3.7 Categorizing application tools is a form of visual note-making

categories for organizing applications on a device to search and find them efficiently. Working with students to create meaningful tags and labels that respond to their specific needs and priorities is a teachable and necessary skill for digital literacy.

It is this ability to organize and interact with material, and then to go on to notate the connections we should try to cultivate in our learners.

A Postscript: Comment-Making on Comments

Students need to be able to react clearly to their notes. It is the comment or question that reflects a student's personal voice, the reaction to the observation that is critical. Students should be encouraged to discuss and share their insights or questions, whether collected on post-its or on a Google doc. Watching the trail of notes develop into a fully developed piece of writing, blog post, or documentary is critical to the learning journey. We should notice our notes.

Conclusion

Extraction of worthy ideas, like mining for gold, requires searching skills. Extraction, by nature, is plodding, but there are critical tools to help. Students should be encouraged to search for meaning and details and then yank them right off the page. The miner takes the findings from a cache and sifts through them while sorting through what is in his pan. In the same fashion, the learner rummages through words, trying to make sense out of what he or she encounters. Critical thinking is a personal reaction to what is found in the search.

Notetaking needs to be reconceived as a creative act. Too often it is viewed as a passive *fetch e*xercise, that is, find the right answer. We need to be clear in our pedagogy that there are multiple sources for notes and that the display of those notes is best viewed in four basic formats. In order for students to reach a degree of mastery in each of these formats, basic notation skills should be developed and practiced in the curriculum.

With the increased ease that our digital capacity provides in maneuvering through both written and visual texts, interactive notetaking and notemaking has grown to be a more natural response. Texting and commenting is easier now. The ability to analyze, choose, and codify confers power. Reaction means acting again. An initial dive into a text is the first action, and then the learner acts again by responding, rejecting, reworking, and eventually creating an investment in learning as he or she creates notes.

Teachers from every discipline can contribute to student success by building creative notetaking strategies for extraction and reaction, as opposed to taking a passive-receptive approach.

4

Editing and Revising Classical Writing and Media Production

A Consistent Developmental Policy to Support Student Independence

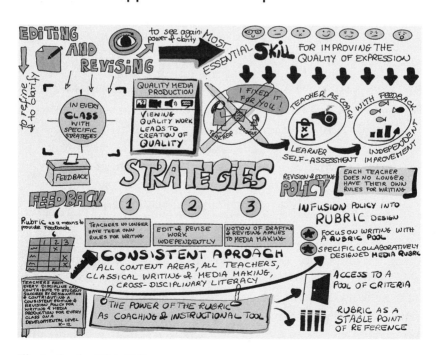

Illustration by Silvia Tolisano

Editing and revising are the most essential skills for improving the quality of our expression, whether in classical writing or in modern media production. However, there are some inherent policy problems that make it challenging for our learners to become independent editors and revisers. We will begin by examining writing and then dive into media production.

So here's how the game is played in writing:

> During first period, I figure out what my math teacher thinks is an "A"; in second period, what my history teacher thinks is an "A"; and in third period, what my Spanish teacher thinks is an "A," and so on and so on. I have to write complete sentences in English, but in social studies and science it depends on who you have. Every year is a new line up. You find out from other kids what each teacher thinks is good work. Some of the teachers edit your work for you. This helps because then you know it will be right. My English teacher can't stand it when our papers are filled with errors, so she fixes them. She gets better and better at editing, but we don't. On the other hand, I don't have to edit my work.
>
> It's kind of interesting because in gym they don't do that. If we are having trouble in basketball making shots, my gym teacher doesn't take the ball out of my hands and make the shot for me. He coaches me. I have to improve my own work in gym, and I'm not even athletic. But, in academics, my teacher fixes my work. Of course, teachers are supposed to do it. Isn't that their job? They should make my work better.

This compilation of quotations from teenagers has the painful ring of truth. In order for students to be able to improve the quality of their work, they have to learn to make their own shots. Practice depends on the concept of revision. The only way that Maria, a budding basketball player, can get better is if she can revise her own shots. Students know, expect, and respect this fundamental concept; and it promotes solid teacher-student relations in the arts as well as in athletics. Both of these fields predicate their pedagogy on the learner making self-assessments and corresponding improvements independently. When a teacher **fixes** Johnny's writing assignment by editing it for him, the paper has been yanked out of Johnny's hand and made better. A corrupting influence develops between student and teacher, for Johnny begins to think, "I am not teachable. You have to fix my paper. You don't think I can fix my paper, so I won't fix my paper." The word *fix* stands out: it implies that a sentence is broken and has to be repaired. If the teacher "fixes" it, the student is not learning much. The teacher is basically taking over as the mechanic while the driver stands to the side. The teacher needs to become a genuine coach, a coach who gives feedback and has the learner make the improvements. As educators, we must accept that these improvements will be gradual.

Johnny will learn more and shape his ideas more effectively if we shift our strategies. Our focus should be on teaching editing and revising in every class with specific, selective, and publicly shared developmental strategies.

I have been asked, "What if the kids don't know how to edit? Don't I need to show them on their papers?" Certainly, a coach demonstrates, but there is a difference between direct teaching and modeling and simply carrying out the work for the learner. A coach assesses if Johnny can make the adjustments to improve his basketball shots. The music teacher assesses whether Rachel can make the necessary changes in her violin performance to work with the string quartet.

The problem is compounded by the fact that many secondary school teachers have received little or no formal training in their own pre-service college education on how to help students read, write, speak, and listen in the subjects that these teachers plan to teach. For example, when a math teacher prepares to teach math, he or she assumes that Johnny knows how to read. It is not surprising, therefore, that when Johnny cannot understand what he reads, the temptation is to blame the English department and the elementary school teachers: "This isn't my job. I'm hired to teach math." Unfortunately, the math teacher cannot be effective in teaching math—in fact, really isn't teaching math—without emphasizing basic language strategies. There is no point in teaching math if Johnny can't process the words. Johnny needs the collective help of all of his teachers in building his language skills. Students need to be taught how to listen, read, edit, and revise.

A genuine revolution in pedagogy has occurred over the past three decades with the widespread acceptance of the writing process K–12 (Graves, 1983; Harwayne, 1987; Calkins, 1994; Atwell, 2002). Using deliberate and thoughtful methods, the remarkable leaders who developed the writer's workshop approach have created a new teaching mentality to support the young, emerging writer. Each child can say, "I am an author; I publish my work; I am a critic; and I have a voice." This chapter does not purport to recapitulate the power of the writing process. What I do want to emphasize in support of that approach is the need for all teachers to collaborate with English and language arts teachers. I am concerned that many of the technical aspects of editing and revision get lost in the curricula of other subjects. The spirit of revision is to see again and to give power and clarity to expression. The spirit of editing is to refine and to clarify so that others can make meaning from our communication. The writing process encourages students to take genuine risks in their self-expression with the use of clearly defined writing tools. In their seminal work, *Infusing Grammar into the Writers Workshop* (2016), Amy Benjamin and Barbara Golub note that within any specific school district there is a range of definitions of grammar compounded by a corresponding range of approaches to teaching it.

In order to build literacy confidence in writing and in speech, learners need to have the technical strategies identified in this chapter developed consistently K–12 in every classroom. They represent a classical, crafted combination of personal voice and technical know-how that creates engaging and meaningful communication. Yet this very classical approach is enhanced dramatically with the inclusion of contemporary digital tools, beginning with those that reside in word processing tools sitting on any computer desktop, laptop, or tablet.

Employing Digital Tools for Feedback to Engage Learners in Editing and Revision

With the advent of word processing tools, in particular Microsoft Word, Mac Pages, and Google Doc, the possibilities for easily providing feedback and commentary to our emerging student writers has proliferated. As you consider the developmental policy suggestions provided for writing to be used throughout a school by all teachers and students, I recommend that there is a concurrent commitment to the use of contemporary feedback and interactive tools. Feedback in and of itself is a critical writing skill, with a power to assist an author while cultivating the insight and observations of the critic. The following are a set of platform-specific recommendations supporting the policy points raised for each developmental level. To be clear, most likely teachers are highly familiar with these tools and functions, yet it is surprising to see how inconsistently they are directly explained to students and used effectively. In many ways, from the student's point of view, it "depends on who you have" as a teacher.

A Proposal for a Consistent Editing and Revision Policy in Classical Writing and Media Making

The following revision and editing policy was developed through input from educators from schools around the United States. It is not carved in stone and might not suit every school setting, but it does provide a touchstone. To implement this policy, all teachers, students, and parents must become familiar with it. They need to understand that these editing and revision skills provide the basis for work in all classes, both in terms of classical writing and media-making production.

Students need to genuinely understand the logic and purpose of grammar. Unfortunately, grammar is often given little attention. When it is taught, the instruction is usually ineffective because educators are far too often unaware of what makes for effective grammar instruction. Typically, grammar is "covered"; it is not learned. When students reach high school, they are usually incapable of speaking about language in any but the most rudimentary terms. Even then, they have little understanding of the concepts governing grammar. Teachers, English teachers included, often struggle with communicating about the nature of grammar and its purpose. It is possible to assist learners in engaging in the logic of grammar and empowering them to become independent writers, in particular through the workshop model (Benjamin and Golub, 2016, p 10).

The following outline establishes appropriate expectations for the development of students' editing and revision skills according to their developmental level. The goal is that each student will eventually learn to work independently on the designated editing and revision tasks at each of these levels:

All Students in Grades K–2 Work Independently:
to edit for:

♦ end punctuation
♦ capitals at the beginning of each sentence
♦ capitals in proper names
♦ complete sentences by reading aloud

to revise for:

♦ replacing one word with a better word

Digital Tool and Media Making Support: Between kindergarten and the second grade learners should know how to navigate basic commands and prompts on either their laptop or tablet to support writing, font selection, and revision. They should know how to save drafts of their writing and begin to employ simple media-making tools such as Storybird or Voicethread.

All Students in Grades 3–5 Work Independently:
to edit for:

♦ end punctuation
♦ internal punctuation for commas
♦ capitalization
♦ subject/verb agreement
♦ proper tense
♦ fuzzy spelling

to revise for:

- descriptive adjectives
- variation in sentence length
- paragraph formation
- engaging openings

Digital Tool and Media Making Support: Between the third and fifth grades students using Microsoft Word or Mac Pages should be taught about the toolbar function under "View" and the role of each symbol, ranging from font selection, size, color, bold, italics, underline, margins, paragraph alignment, sentence spacing, and highlighting. They should be working with media-making platforms that populate their hardware, such as iMovie with Macs or Chromebook and Google apps. Voice-over on fundamental projects using PowerPoint, Keynote, or Prezi type presentations should be emphasized, with a focus on editing for best quality.

All Students in Grades 6–8 Work Independently in All Subjects:
to edit for:

- end punctuation
- internal punctuation (comma, semicolon, colon, quotation marks)
- all capitalization
- complete sentences
- run-on sentences and sentence fragments
- subject-verb agreement
- proper tense

to revise for:

- precise and rich vocabulary, with a focus on including adjectives and adverbs, more engaging action verbs, and more precise nouns
- sentence variety
- paragraph formation

Digital Tools and Media Making Support: All students in middle school should be expected to create more sophisticated and specific media genre for projects. In other words, rather than a "video clip," they might create an animated short or a documentary. Accompanying these media projects requires the viewing of quality examples and the integration of more sophisticated digital tools such as ScreenFlow, the development and insertion of avatars, and green screen productions.

All Students in Grades 9–12 Work Independently in Each Class:
to edit for:

♦ end punctuation
♦ internal punctuation (comma, semicolon, colon, quotation marks)
♦ all capitalization
♦ complete sentences
♦ run-on sentences and sentence fragments
♦ subject-verb agreement
♦ proper tense

to revise for:

♦ precise and rich vocabulary, with a focus on including adjectives and adverbs, more engaging action verbs, and more precise nouns
♦ sentence variety
♦ paragraph formation
♦ smooth transitions
♦ expansive openings
♦ including concessions in arguments
♦ appropriate voice
♦ expanded range in genre choices

Digital Tools and Media Making Support: High school–level learners should be engaged in opportunities to read and write screenplays for both narrative and documentary media projects. It is easy to locate a free downloadable copy of a screenplay online for any major or even smaller scale film. The opportunity to use a range of media-making platforms and tools can be coordinated between departments so that each academic year a major outcome would be a film or short animated project. For example, the history department requires that students create a documentary to persuade viewers on a point of view on a global issue. The earth science department requires that students use the media-making tool Animoto to demonstrate the movement of the earth's plates from Pangea to the present and then onto the future. Media production specialists can be a great asset when they work with classroom teachers, but what needs to be avoided is having students who only sign up for a film-making elective have the opportunity. Rather than viewing media making as an enrichment opportunity, it should be viewed as requisite.

So now the game changes. Each teacher no longer has his or her own rules for writing, and Johnny no longer has to figure out what those rules are. Instead, everyone plays by the same rules and has the same expectations. Johnny must learn to edit and revise his work independently. What is more, he will be expected to bring this notion of drafting and editing and revising to media-making projects. If he struggles with the writing skills, the primary responsibility for direction falls on the English teacher, whose task is to provide effective instruction in both grammar and rhetoric. English is "base camp for applied grammar." Other subject area teachers cannot abdicate their responsibility to provide direct teaching and coaching, but certainly it is the language arts/English curriculum that is best suited for direct instruction. It is the subsequent responsibility of all other teachers to follow through, grade, and give feedback to Johnny not only on the content of his work, but also on his technical ability to convey it. In terms of media making, the teacher introducing the tools and approach is inherently responsible to follow through with support. Central is the notion that the teacher and the students draft collaborative rubrics in advance of making a media project so that they can truly learn together. Key is a consistent approach to editing and revision, whether classical writing or media production.

Cross-disciplinary literacy expectations should be consistent and clear, and supported by families as well. They can be posted on a school's website. In addition, teachers can create short video mini-lessons on critical editing and revision coaching points. Students would then be able to review critical points related to the logic and role of writing with examples and follow-up exercises.

By adhering to and supporting this public policy, teachers are requesting that students become active editors and revisers at an age-appropriate level. For example, one first grade teacher asks students to pretend that they are driving their "sentence cars" as they write. When Maria approaches the end of the "street," she needs to let her readers know that they need to stop. Her teacher reinforces the concept by having Maria stick a little round red sticker, the period, as a kind of stop sign. Her teacher says, "Now, Maria, to let your readers know they are about to go down a new sentence street, what might we do to give them a signpost?" Maria responds, "We make the first letter a capital. We make it big to let the reader know something new is coming." This first grade teacher is conveying the actual logic of the punctuation and capitalization with her developmental teaching. The logic is to alert the reader to the end of sentences and the beginnings of new ones. Of greater importance is that through this exercise Maria begins to understand that logic too. Perhaps high school students should be introduced to the notion of "speed bumps" to correct their tendency to use run-on sentences.

It should be clear that there is a direct link between writing and the other language capacities of speaking, listening, and reading, and that this linkage is at the heart of improving Johnny's power with the pen. As Amy Benjamin notes in her seminal work, *Writing in the Content Areas* (2005):

Writing is the most intellectually demanding of the four modes of communication through language. Writing is the last of the four to be mastered. First we learn to understand spoken language; then, we learn to produce it through speech. Long after that, and usually only with a great deal of time and effort, do we learn to decode symbols and develop enough fluency to make meaning from them. But writing, encoding, has an even more sophisticated component than reading: writers have to figure out that writing conventions are stricter than those for speech. Fledgling writers often proclaim, "I write the way I speak." What they should be doing, however, is writing the way they read.

Obviously, writing is only going to be as good as it is substantial. Writers need a message. Before we expect students to be able to write anything about our subject, we have to see to it that they've read in the subject area. Conceive of writing as one of the four language components and understand the interdependency of the reading, writing, listening, and speaking.

The process of speaking is, for many learners, a process of speaking oneself into knowing. The learner may have to put the words in his or her own mouth to internalize the concepts. Hence, a classroom consisting predominantly of teacher talk will result in an imbalance in the four language components. Think of it as driving a car in only first gear.

(p. 5)

Infusing the Policy Into Rubric Design

The use of rubrics is widespread as a means of providing feedback to students on their work. The Latin derivation of rubric is "to highlight in red" and comes from the practice in monasteries when monks would use red calligraphy to feature passages in liturgical texts. The essence of the root meaning is compelling. We are looking for rubrics to highlight and provide feedback, not to make wrong. There are two approaches to rubrics that I advocate. The first we will consider focuses on writing with the development of a *rubric pool*. The second strategy is for the development of a specific, collaboratively designed media rubric determined directly by the nature of the product and the tool to be used.

A Writing Rubric Pool

Because of the shift to more writing assessment in all subjects, classroom teachers at all levels of instruction are expected to adhere to the rubric as an evaluation tool for their learners. The same holds true on some of our national examinations. For example, the new writing section of the College Boards' SAT 2005 has altered the scoring potential from a possible 1600 points to 2400 points. This shift in emphasis reflects the pervasive view that our learners need to become more effective writers. And there is a generic rubric used to assist learners nationally on the examination. The College Board's seminal report, *The Neglected "R": The Need for a Writing Revolution*, by the National Commission on Writing (2003), notes:

> Writing is everybody's business . . . guidelines should require writing in every curriculum area and all grade levels. Writing opportunities that are developmentally appropriate should be provided to every student, from the earliest years through secondary school into college. Common expectations about writing should be developed across disciplines through in-service workshops designed to help teachers understand good writing and develop as writers themselves.
>
> (p. 6)

Potential problems emerge when educators attempt to improve students' editing and revision skills through the use of some of these broad rubrics. A dedicated faculty, however, can assist learners and improve cross-disciplinary literacy in all classes. If these problems are not addressed, the state (or national) testing rubric may seem to be at cross purposes, because a state or national rubric purporting application for every child is by nature broad and sweeping. Educators should adapt and rework these rubrics for their own student population. In addition, a rubric used after the fact, rather than as an antecedent to any writing, reduces its effectiveness. Post-writing use of a rubric diminishes the power of the rubric as a coaching and instructional tool. If Abdul knows in advance what quality writing is in a very specific way, he can revise and improve his work accordingly.

One way to address this problem is to make certain that the classroom rubric used with a student population is based on the editing and revising policy cited earlier in the chapter. At the same time, teachers can literally draw a one-to-one correspondence between the targeted editing and revision strategies and the broader state rubrics. Here is an example of how to refine a state rubric:

> The state writing rubric, which says that the student should *use language to communicate effectively*, is far too general and is, in fact, not teachable. It should be refined into an observable teaching action. An effective school writing policy or classroom rubric might say that the student should *revise sentences to include descriptive adjectives*.

When a generalized rubric is revised for greater specificity, Abdul knows precisely what he needs to do. The inclusion of more vivid and descriptive adjectives will certainly enable him to meet the broader statewide criteria of using language to communicate effectively.

Another problem is that students are inundated with rubrics. They are, in a sense, "rubriced out." They are overwhelmed and confused by too many rubrics.

If teachers had access to a pool of criteria, we could establish a cross-disciplinary solution to a school-wide problem (see Table 4.1). All teachers could use that long list of potential criteria in a focused way. They would never use all of the criteria at one time. The pool would be available for selective use. A science teacher might choose to focus on using supporting details and developing a thesis statement for one paper, whereas the art teacher might be working with establishing point of view and revising for word choice on another paper. The important factor is that the pool of criteria would remain stable and common among every faculty member and every student. Consider the following example:

TABLE 4.1 High School/Middle School Writing Rubric

Criteria/Definitions	4	3	2	1
Content—The extent to which the paper exhibits sound understanding, interpretation, and analysis of the task and text				
Introduction of thesis	Thesis insightful and clearly stated Key terms defined Introduction energizing	Thesis stated Some key terms defined Introduction interesting	Thesis vague Terms not defined Introduction not clear	No thesis stated No terms defined No introduction provided
Opening	Clear focus on topic Thorough introduction of topic Powerful message conveyed to reader	Topic introduced Sufficient focus on topic Message conveyed to reader	Little focus on topic and purpose Vague message conveyed to reader	No focus on topic No message conveyed to reader
Development of ideas	Interesting, sophisticated, insightful Strongly supports thesis	Development of ideas clear, evident, and supportive of thesis	Simplistic. Does not support thesis Varying in quality	Absent or ineffective
Supporting evidence and details	Uses examples, reasons, explanations, etc., that are relevant, appropriate, and convincing	Examples, reasons, details, and explanations sufficient and accurate	Some examples, reasons, details, etc., sufficient and accurate	Vague, missing, inaccurate evidence
Conclusion	Extends, connects, comments on key ideas and topics	Summarizes main ideas; echoes key concepts	Restates main idea	Absent, incomplete, or unfocused

Development—The extent to which the response exhibits direction, shape, coherence

Sentence variety (word choice, word order, sentence length)	Well varied sentence structure throughout piece	Evidence of some sentence variety	Occasional sentence variety	No sentence variety
Paragraph development	Each paragraph clearly and consistently relates to the main idea, contributes to an effective argument, and reinforces the content; smooth transitions.	Many paragraphs relate to main idea, contribute to an effective argument, and reinforce the content; often uses smooth transitions.	Some paragraphs relate to main idea, contribute to an effective argument, and have smooth transitions.	No or few paragraphs relate to main idea, contribute to an effective argument or have smooth transitions.
Organization with pre-set	Requirements of format are met consistently throughout piece.	Many of the requirements of format are met in the piece.	Some of the requirements of format are met in the piece.	Few or none of the requirements for the format are met.
Designing organization	Creates an organizational pattern that effectively supports the topic/thesis of the piece	Creates an organizational pattern that adequately supports the topic/thesis of the piece	Creates an organizational pattern that inconsistently supports the topic/thesis of the piece	Little or no organizational pattern to support the topic/thesis of the piece
Narrative Craft				
Story structure	Establishes a strong plot, conflict, climax, setting, and point of view. Develops an effective blend of dialogue, narration, and action	Establishes plot, conflict, climax, setting, and point of view. Develops a mostly effective blend of dialogue, narration, and action	Some elements of story structure are present and/or weak blending of dialogue, narration, and action.	Few or no story structure elements are present and/or no blending of dialogue, narration, or action is present.

(Continued)

TABLE 4.1 High School/Middle School Writing Rubric (Continued)

Criteria/Definitions	4	3	2	1
Characterization	Develops complex characters through effective blend of dialogue, narration, and action	Develops characters through a blend of dialogue, narration, and action	There is some character development through dialogue, narration, and/or action.	Characters are not developed. Doesn't blend dialogue, narration, and action
Description	Creates vivid "pictures" through concrete language and rich sensory detail; use of metaphor, simile, analogies, and other literary devices; incorporates the five senses	Creates "pictures" through concrete language and sensory detail; uses many literary devices, and incorporates sensory detail	Some use of concrete language and sensory detail; uses some literary devices and/or sensory detail	Uses little or no concrete language and sensory detail
Word choice	Uses appropriate, sophisticated, precise vocabulary There is a clear sense of audience.	Uses many effective and appropriate words A sense of audience is evident.	Uses some effective and appropriate words There is some sense of audience.	Uses few or no correct or effective words There is little or no sense of audience.

Conventions—The extent to which the response exhibits conventional spelling, punctuation, paragraphing, capitalization, grammar, and usage.

Criteria/Definitions	4	3	2	1
Punctuation	Exhibits correct grammar in each sentence Smooth, fluid sentences No run-ons or fragments Error-free punctuation	Exhibits mostly correct grammar Errors in punctuation do not interfere with communication.	Exhibits errors in grammar that somewhat interfere with communication	Exhibits errors in grammar that interfere with communication throughout

Spelling and usage	Exhibits correct spelling and usage Error free	Exhibits mostly correct spelling and usage	Exhibits errors in spelling and usage that somewhat interfere with communication	Exhibits errors in spelling and usage that interfere with communication Misspelled/misused words throughout
Presentation	Neat and professional, clean presentation; shows attention to details	Neat, easy to read	Sometimes hard to read; careless presentation	Little or no attention to presentation
Meaning—The extent to which the response exhibits sound understanding, interpretation, and analysis of the task and texts. These criteria are particularly central to informational and analytic writing.				
Accuracy of response	Arrives at correct responses consistently through correct and appropriate computations	Arrives at correct responses most of the time If the response is incorrect, it is the result of a minor error.	Arrives at correct responses some of the time A few of the responses may be incorrect because of major errors.	Arrives at incorrect responses because of major errors in computation
Conceptual understanding	Shows a depth of understanding of concept with ample support	Shows understanding with adequate support	Shows some understanding with some support	Understanding not evident
Explanation of reasoning	Provides a clear, coherent, complete and organized explanation of math concepts and/or problem-solving strategies	Provides a clear and organized explanation of math concepts and/or problem-solving strategies	Provides a general explanation which is organized but lacking in details	Provides an unclear or incomplete explanation of the problem-solving process Major steps or concepts may be omitted.

(Continued)

TABLE 4.1 High School/Middle School Writing Rubric (Continued)

Criteria/Definitions	4	3	2	1
Data collection	Accurately displays data in both table and graph formats. Data is thorough, and includes values, labels, titles, appropriate scaling, and best-fit line.	Data is reasonable and includes most of the values, labels, titles, appropriate scaling, and a best-fit line.	Accurately displays data in both table and graph formats Includes sufficient values, labels, titles, and scales to demonstrate comprehension	Inaccurately displays data in table and/or graph formats Data is not reasonable and/or significant details are missing that interfere with comprehension.
Data analysis	Precisely states hypothesis and accurately compares hypothesis to the actual results Presents ample detail and data to support thesis statement Accurately and thoroughly explains and states the type of relationship between input (independent) and outcome (dependent) variables	Clearly states hypothesis and accurately compares hypothesis to the actual results Presents sufficient data to support thesis statement Accurately explains and states the type of relationship between input (independent) and outcome (dependent) variables	Accurately compares hypothesis to the actual results Generally refers to the data to support this relationship Accurately explains or states the relationship between input (independent) and outcome (dependent) variables	Inaccurately compares proposed explanation/ hypothesis to the actual results Does not refer or present data to support this relationship Inaccurately states the type of relationship between input (dependent) variables as indicated by the data
Evaluation	Provides a meaningful, precise, and complete explanation of strengths and weaknesses of the work	Provides a complete explanation of strengths and weaknesses of the work	Provides a meaningful but partial explanation of strong and weak points of the work	Provides an incomplete explanation of the strengths and weaknesses of the work
Implications and suggested improvements	Provides clear, powerful, specific, and logical discussion of the improvements that could be made	Provides a specific and logical discussion of the improvements that could be made	Provides a general but logical discussion of the improvements that could be made	Provides an unclear and/ or illogical discussion of the improvements that could be made

There is no second guessing the standard. Teachers can tailor and focus the students' work, but they cannot confuse them with blurry standards any longer. A math teacher may draw from four or five criteria that are different from an English teacher's criteria, yet they all come from the same source. The rubric provides a stable point of reference so that the learner can increase his internalized judgment with precision.

Of equal importance, the broad and sweeping state rubrics used for gauging test results are not only fulfilled but also deepened with the greater specificity of the language used in the indicators. A consistent approach, as well as a consistent policy, assists students in all situations where they need to be independent editors of their own work.

There is a natural flow to the creation of the young writer. Worsham (2001) writes,

> To write successfully, students—and all of us—need to begin with personal writing for self. Writing for self means loosening up: freewriting; journal keeping; and concrete, self-centered writing. . . . The next step in writing is to reach out to others. Often writing during this stage is characterized by letters and notes written to a perceived audience—friends, parents, teachers—from whom a response is anticipated. As this stage progresses, the writer becomes more aware of his audience. And only last should students learn to write expository, more abstract kinds of writing, including persuasive essays, newspaper articles, or research papers. . . . In this third stage, the most distant audience from self, the writer is more concerned with a relationship with a subject.

Ultimately, formal assessments should be based on whether Maria, Johnny, Abdul, and Rachel can independently improve the quality of their own writing without teacher interference. It is inherently unfair to criticize students for their inconsistency when there are wide variations on standards of editing and revision among teachers within and between grades and departments. The essential strategy here requires a degree of trust and commitment among classroom teachers. The unique roles of teachers of the language arts, English, and ESL are clear. What also needs to be clarified is the responsibility of all other staff to support the students as they journey from subject to subject trying to build their independent writing capacity.

Media Production: Collaborative Rubric Design for Editing and Revising

Building on the premise of feedback and standards setting in classical writing, the development of meaningful media is similarly based on a recognition of what makes a quality production. Given that so few teachers have had formal background in media production, it is not surprising that there is a tendency for student to literally be "left to their own devices." Eyebrows should be raised when a group of elementary or middle school students are running around a school yard with flip cameras making movies. The care and consideration that goes into a classical approach to a first draft in writing is predicated on a study of technical aspects of writing, expert employment of elements, and authenticity to the voice of the writer. I advocate for two strategies that can support a school-wide and consistent approach to quality media production:

1. The focused study on models of success in media production.
2. The cultivation of collaboratively developed media rubrics between teachers and students completed in advance of media production.

Just as the study of great writing can inspire authentic and well-crafted expression in our students, so does the study of quality media. In short, viewing quality work leads to the creation of quality. For the classroom teacher, the viewing of a selected media genre should be done with an eye to developing a sense of what makes a work a great one. As noted in *Mastering Media Literacy* (2014), Frank W. Baker and I make a case for creating a film canon of valued works for schools to reference in our chapter titled "Designing a Film Study Curriculum and Canon" (pp. 80–81), with the notion that if teachers trust a vetted set of well-regarded film work as we do in literature there would be an appreciable increase in the formal study of media. We have also developed a website filled with film resources that have been organized around film types and sorted by age group, titled the Film Canon Project (http://filmcanonproject.com) for teachers and students to draw upon in their study.

Central is the creation of collaboratively designed media production rubrics by teachers and learners working together after viewing excellent media examples. Questions emerge for discussion: What makes a quality film? Why does this documentary seem so compelling? There will be both technical and content criteria when shaping the rubric.

In media production rubric design attention can be given to:

- ◆ technical aspects of creating a media genre, such as framing an image, sound quality, color, lighting, wide angle, and zoom-in perspectives
- ◆ elements of story telling or documenting via image sequences, voice-over, and dialogue
- ◆ authenticity of purpose behind a documentary or the voice of the author in a narrative piece
- ◆ genre match of media type, whether it is short or long documentary, narrative story, or animated

Fundamentally, students need to be steeped in the *language of film* (Jacobs and Baker, 2014) and should be conscious of the operational meaning of terms such as:

- ◆ Camera (lens, positioning, and movement)
- ◆ Lights
- ◆ Sound (including music and sound effects)
- ◆ Set design
- ◆ Post-production (editing)
- ◆ Acting (including expression, body language, costume, and make-up)

For our purposes and in the spirit of editing and revising strate-gies in writing, media editing and revision is also the place where a first draft is shaped and re-worked to become a more mean-ingful entity. The central difference is reflected in the previously mentioned terms, that is, our students are now adding sound and possibly the visual to the product. Should the terms *editing and revising* keep the definition shared here for writing? With media work, editing takes on both the correction of technical issues (the sound is not clear enough) as well as the revision to improve quality. Media editing deal with shortening or lengthening a scene, reconsidering angles on a subject, re-sequencing images or voice-over, or employing visual effects such as lighting. With so many additional considerations for generating quality media productions, it is no wonder that teachers might be reluctant to support media products or to capitulate to mediocre first drafts as acceptable. Yet, I would argue that we must choose our century—in fact, most of what we call film media came from the last century—and it is time we caught up right now with learners and their need to shape and study contemporary media concurrently with classical written expression.

A developmental policy for editing and revision in both clas-sical writing and media production can be a significant guide in a learner's journey from early childhood through graduation.

Teachers from every discipline can contribute to student success by designating and employing a consistent editing and revision policy for writing and media production for every class on a developmental level K–12.

5

Face to Face in Real and Virtual Space

Speaking, Listening, and Discussion Types

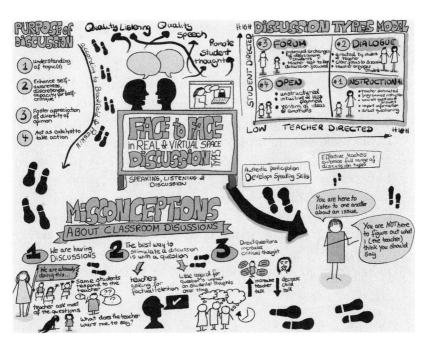

Illustration by Silvia Tolisano

The Latin root of "discussion" is *discutere*, meaning to shake apart. When students speak about ideas in a public forum, and when they react to and rattle ideas around, it is an act of ownership and investment. In some classroom environments, however, speaking is an act of courage. By listening to others, we can infuse our own thoughts with associations, reactions, and suggestions. When we hear ourselves out loud and get a response from others, there is the possibility of feedback and engagement. The problem with most classroom discussion is that all too often it is a great opportunity that is missed. Too often discussion is canned and dominated by a teacher who leads a handful of habitual hand-raisers. Just as there can be static writing in school assignments, there can be inauthentic and stilted discussion. What passes for discussion is actually Q&A, where the teacher plays "Guess what I'm thinking." This scenario can be countered with a different approach to and strategy for classroom discussion. Discussions have the exciting possibility for broaching the unknown and the unpredictable response from a student, and can provide an impetus for inquiry. Brookfield and Peskill (2005) provide an engaging and practical definition:

> We define discussion as an alternately serious and playful effort by a group of two or more to share views and engage in mutual and reciprocal critique. The purposes of discussion are fourfold: (1) to help participants reach a more critically informed understanding about the topic or topics under consideration, (2) to enhance participants' self-awareness, discreteness and their capacity for self-critique, (3) to foster an appreciation among participants or the diversity of opinion that invariably emerges when viewpoints are exchanged openly and honestly, and (4) to act as a catalyst to helping people take informed action in the world.
>
> (p. 6)

Whatever the intended purpose on the part of the teacher or student in a discussion, we now have the opportunity for a refreshed view of interaction with our ability to have virtual discussions with video conferencing and webcasting platforms.

These formats raise new questions: Do best practices for an on-site discussion apply to a virtual one? Are there times when a virtual discussion might be preferred to an on-site experience? The prospect for changing the nature of classroom interaction is exciting. We can replace present practices with more effective strategies. We need to re-conceptualize the nature of discussion; thus I propose a model for discussion types to clarify various kinds of discussion and the inherent value of each type. The purpose of this model is to improve the performance of our learners, to engage them in meaningful interactions, and to increase their confidence as speakers and listeners. To set the stage for the model, let us begin by examining misconceptions about discussions and then considering a proposed Discussion Types Model adapted for both on-site and virtual interactions.

Misconceptions About Classroom Discussion

At its best, classroom discussion allows learners to *shake apart* ideas so that they can put ideas together in new and better ways. In order to revitalize speaking across the disciplines, this chapter identifies three fundamental misconceptions about discussion that are major obstacles to successful classroom communication. These misconceptions dampen the liveliness of classrooms and create a predictable lethargy. To counter this malaise, the Discussion Types Model is presented with corresponding instructional strategies to increase the quality and quantity of classroom interactions.

Misconception 1: We Are Having Discussions

We rarely have classroom discussions. The word *discussion* may appear in a teacher's plan books, but when it comes time to implement that strategy, chances are the teacher only plays puppeteer. The teacher asks a question of one student, nods, then asks another question of another student, nods, then asks a question of another student, and then proceeds to answer the questions. There is limited student-to-student interaction, and the responses will probably be less than five words. As a field we have decades of research on the nature of classroom interaction. In most of these studies, classroom discussions were first taped and then analyzed word for word. The analyses considered variables such as the number of student-versus-teacher initiated questions, the length of teacher talk versus the length of student talk through a word count, the numbers of students who participated, and the regularity of each student's participation (Evans, 1970; Bellack, 1966; Dillon, 1988).

The findings suggest that there are a handful of "designated hitters" in each class. These are the same students who always respond to the teacher. In a sense, there is a degree of collusion where both teachers and students covertly agree about who the speakers will be. One of the most striking findings from classroom interaction analyses is that the teacher will most likely ask all of the questions. Chances are slim that a student will initiate a question, and, even when the question is asked, it likely is a clarification question such as "Is this what you want?" Although our intention is to encourage critical thinking, present teaching practices generally inhibit student thought in discussion (Dillon, 1988).

Misconception 2: The Best Way to Stimulate Discussion Is with a Question

If one were to ask most teachers the best way to ascertain what a child is thinking, the likely answer would be, "Ask him." There is no doubt that questions are overused. When they are used, it is with little regard for their impact on student thought over time. Teachers initiate about 80% of all classroom questions (Bellack, 1966; Dillon, 1988), and this high incidence of teacher-initiated questions ultimately limits student thought at a time when they should be seeking information. Furthermore, 80% of all of the questions that teachers ask are on the recall level, the lowest level of questioning (Bellack, 1966). In short, teachers do almost all of the asking, and what they are asking for is factual retention.

A question is a cue. Within the syntax of the question's phrasing is a message that tells the student the level of thought expected in response and the parameters for an exchange of ideas. If the teacher asks for low-level responses, the student responds in kind. In other words, displays of knowledge, comprehension, and application (Bloom, 1956) are the most commonly requested levels of thinking. Within the structure of the question is the most revealing cue component, the verb. When teachers pose questions that use verbs such as "tell," "state," "list," or "define," they are clearly requesting recall of facts. If, on the other hand, the instructor cues the higher levels of thinking, i.e., analysis, synthesis, and evaluation (Bloom, 1956), one is more likely to hear such verbs as "disassemble," "deduce," "combine," "create," "design," or "appraise." In short, what you ask for is what you get.

Many educators attempt to use cognitive models to encourage critical thinking in the classroom. These models are appropriate and meaningful when applied to problems worth pursuing. As we consider a model for encouraging thought expressed through discussion, it is important to consider the full range of types of interaction. There are classroom situations in which direct questioning is a valuable tool. Although direct questioning is not appropriate for certain types of discussion, it is helpful in a few specific situations.

Misconception 3: Direct Questions Increase Critical Thought

Over the decades the research outlining the negative effect of direct questions on student thought has been provocative (Dillon, 1978, 1988). Most of this work supports the thesis that direct questions depress thinking in students. Teacher-initiated questions are often a form of control. Such questions encourage students to take on the role of completing the classroom script rather than voicing authentic opinions. Dillon's (1978, 1988) work clearly indicates that although teachers may claim to want their children to speak openly in class, the opposite actually occurs. Even though teachers claim to desire a discussion, their questions actually decrease child-talk and increase teacher-talk.

Let me clarify by offering an analogy to a dinner party. At a dinner party, the social expectation is that people will exchange ideas and feelings in an open manner. If the host sits at the head of the table and directly questions each person around the table, the results are hardly deemed a discussion, let alone the social event of the season. Discussions simply do not occur in overly controlled situations. In asking directive questions, the teacher is using an instructional mode that does not encourage the high level of reflection we encourage in discussion. This is not to say that a discussion is a free-for-all. The teacher has a specific role to play, but research indicates that teachers who ask direct questions discourage interaction between students and tend to put a ceiling on the level of abstraction that occurs in the interaction.

A student response to a teacher question is short, usually a single word or phrase. When teachers increase their rate of questioning, there is a direct correlation with low rates of voluntary responses from students. Students tend to give short and simple answers to teacher questions in discussions; in fact, appreciable proportions of teacher-initiated questions receive no student response at all. Significantly, student responses to questions from other students are longer and more complete than responses to teacher questions. Dillon (1978, 1988) finds it hard to escape the conclusion that direct questioning inhibits the number and the nature of student responses. As Yamada (1913) asserted over one hundred years ago, to rely on a question "is to make children passive and halting in their self-expression and independent mental activity" (p. 147).

I believe these inhibiting practices cast the student into the role of a witness being "badgered" by the teacher, even when there is a nice tone in the teacher's voice. Students are conditioned to believe that direct questioning is for right and wrong answers. A direct question is simply not effective in a discussion. Alternatives such as silence and declarative statements (Dillon, 1988) can replace the question.

Students receive a new and powerful set of cues when a shift in syntax occurs. The message is clear when the teacher explains: "You are here to listen to one another about an issue. You are *not* here to figure out what I (the teacher) think you should say." With such an approach, the students are off the witness stand and truly facing one another.

The Discussion Types Model

As a remedy for the three misconceptions, the teaching model presented here is designed to create a dynamic and meaningful opportunity for students to develop speaking skills. Some real tensions often discourage teachers from encouraging authentic and widespread participation in discussions. In spontaneous and meaningful discussions, people do call out impulsively, overstay their welcome, run off focus, and break out into side conversations. It is this messiness that deters teachers from going there. They might feel better about taking risks if they understand that a loss of some control is inevitable, and that true discussion in a classroom involves relinquishing some control in exchange for an exciting, meaningful class. Through the use of proper cues and tools, teachers can create new confidence and control on the part of their learners. In addition, maybe because students are not used to it, they are likely to regard a class with lively discussion as a class in which "we didn't do anything today." Careful structuring, as well as clear communication with our students about expectations, allows us to ward off that perception. Finally, a sense of community is necessary in any attempt to build powerful speaking and listening skills. The use of a model of discussion types, I believe, can cultivate that dynamic and caring community.

The Discussion Types Model that I propose here defines four types of discussion. I identify each type and describe situations where it is best applied and the cues that are most conducive to its effective use. Two assumptions govern the use of this model: (1) that no one type is best and (2) that the effective teacher embraces the full range of discussion types and is able to diagnose the situation best served by any one of the types. Teachers in all disciplines and at all levels of instruction can adapt and apply this model. In response to our need to focus on contemporary learning environments, I will describe both on-site classical discussion and the implications for virtual learning platforms. Figure 5.1 shows the various types of discussion. Each quadrant indicates the degree of teacher-directed behavior and student-directed behavior in discussion, with varying emphasis on either teacher- or student-directed behaviors. Definitions and corresponding cues follow.

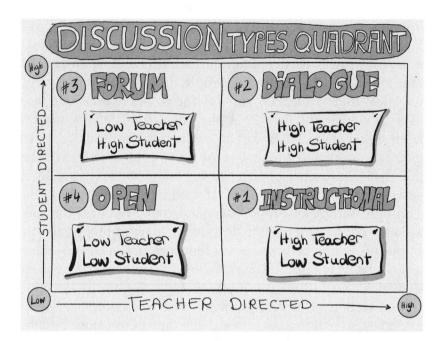

FIGURE 5.1 Discussion Types Model (illustration by Silvia Tolisano)

Quadrant 1: Instructional Discussion (High Teacher, Low Student)

Definition: This type of classroom interaction is highly teacher dominated in terms of talk and control. It is akin to programmed instruction. The teacher asks a concrete question and expects a specific answer. Although it differs from a lecture, which is totally teacher talk, the intent is much the same. The teacher wishes to impart information and solicits direct responses from students to assess their assimilation of the information. Effective direct questioning using a taxonomy (Bloom, 1956, is essential in this quadrant). This is an important teaching method and, undoubtedly, is the most commonly used type.

Cues: The teacher cues student behavior by specifying the objectives for the instructional period and clarifying that they should respond either by raising their hands or giving another nonverbal signal. The teacher is explicit about his or her need to assess the student's understanding of the material through direct questioning. By the same token, the teacher informs the students of the level of thinking desired in this exchange. If the dominant mode is recall or information, students are cued to draw from the data, which they have memorized. If the teacher gives instruction through direct questioning on an application level (Bloom, 1956), then students think in terms of using the data to demonstrate competence. The instructional discussion reflects the first three levels of Bloom's taxonomy.

Virtual Considerations: When a student responds to a carefully orchestrated online learning course and responds to direct cues from a teacher, it is akin to the same type of interaction on-site in a classroom. A webinar devoted to direct teaching is an example of how a virtual instructional discussion is featured.

Quadrant 2: Dialogue Discussion (High Teacher, High Student)

Definition: This type of interaction is highly directed by both the teacher and the students because it is a mutual interaction. There is a clear focus to the discussion, and the role of the teacher is to actively engage students in examining various issues that relate to the focus. The Socratic method falls into this quadrant. The teacher does have an agenda, but a large part of that agenda is to direct students to appraise ideas critically. Questions serve the purpose of guiding students toward analysis, although non-questioning strategies are equally effective. Students are encouraged to raise genuine questions.

Cues: The cues given to students are formal. The teacher directs students to respond with higher levels of thinking such as analysis, synthesis, and evaluation (Bloom, 1956). In a sense, the teacher is saying, "We are going to examine concepts or issues in a direct exchange. I will pose issues requiring you to reflect on your positions and to consider the consequences of your view." The students must understand that the teacher's role is to encourage them to critically appraise a range of perspectives, and the teacher must clearly state his or her role in this discussion. In this type of discussion, teachers follow up on student responses with more essential questions: "What are the specific reasons for your position? What are the consequences of your position?" When students learn to take responsibility for their beliefs, they become true critical thinkers. Unless this occurs, we run the risk of the old-school game in which students try to say what "sounds good" to the teacher's ears. The cue must be precise: "In this class, if you want 'to please the teacher,' state your mind, support your view, and own the results."

Virtual Consideration: Clearly the opportunity for give and take are particularly possible with one-to-one interactions using video conferencing such as FaceTime, Skype, or Google Hangout. The most dynamic plus is the potential expansion to global dialogues with individuals anywhere there is access. It is recommended that the recording feature on a platform be employed to review the dialogue afterwards. In particular, virtual interactions are restricted in terms of the awareness of others in physical setting.

Quadrant 3: Forum Discussion (Low Teacher, High Student)

Definition: This type of interaction encourages prolonged exchanges of ideas among students. The focus of discussion is stated, and the teacher's task is to keep the discussion focused. The teacher is not a primary participant in the flow of expressed viewpoints. In my experience, the Forum Discussion is the least likely to occur and the most subtle to manage. Students must be well prepared on the topic at hand, and the teacher must be willing to restrain the tendency to intervene.

Cues: Students hear cues for this discussion type that may be quite new to them. The teacher explicitly requests that students speak directly to one another, listen carefully to their peers, and exchange ideas on the issue at hand. The teacher should remind them that (1) there is a topic to be scrutinized and that (2) there is a discussion procedure to be learned. For this type of discussion to be successful, students must be prepared, prior to the forum, with both factual information and the ability to articulate their views. They need to have something of substance to say. Another cue for students is the role of the teacher, who acts as a listener and who raises a point only if the exchanges grossly leave the topic. Non-questioning cues (such as restatements) are critical to the success of this type of discussion.

Virtual Considerations: When setting up a forum virtually it is important to select a platform that will allow for interaction between parties. For example, Google Hangout and Skype allow for multiple individuals to see one another and to interact. Rules for engagement should be established at the beginning so that there are respectful pauses when someone wishes to speak, if not a hand signal, given that it is more challenging to read body language in a virtual setting. Clearly the invitation to participate in a virtual forum should relate directly to the topic or issue under investigation and the perspective that each participant brings to the "virtual table." Because recording is possible, it can be of great value for individuals to review the interaction to determine critical focal points in the discussion.

Quadrant 4: Open Discussion (Low Teacher, Low Student)

Definition: Because the last type of discussion is the most unstructured, it is called "the open discussion." The group follows a more intuitive and less planned direction as both the teacher and the students vent ideas and emotions. There are situations in school life where a group needs to unload without the formal constraints of a directed lesson. Perhaps an event on the playground or in the larger world warrants immediate discussion. These are genuine learning moments and opportunities. The teacher can encourage participation and set the tone for appropriate consideration of others. For the open discussion to take place, students must have a high level of trust in the teacher and feel safe within their classroom community, and the teacher must be willing to yield to the teachable moment. Ultimately, these exchanges, in themselves, work to build a supportive classroom community.

Cues: The cues are those of encouragement and limit setting. The teacher makes it clear that there is a presenting need that requires a response. The teacher encourages the class members to express thoughts and feelings while, at the same time, clearly setting limits that avoid personal attacks or that prohibit any one individual from dominating the discussion. The teacher also must think through his or her role as well. It may be necessary for him or her to express a point of view while avoiding the tendency to take over the discussion and turn it into a lecture.

Virtual implications: Because the open discussion is an unplanned event in response to a specific situation, virtual open discussions often occur in social networks away from the school environment. In a classroom situation, if there is an ongoing relationship with another school, class, individual, organization, or network, it is possible that a teacher may say "Let's check in with our partners or friends to get their point of view" in a spontaneous fashion.

Through my work with teachers in putting the model into practice in the classroom, I have found that, in practice, the discussion types may overlap. A lesson may begin as a dialogue, then merge into a forum as students gather momentum in discussing the issue at hand. During a dialogue discussion, the teacher may feel that students need more instructional support and shift to the instructional mode of the first quadrant. The framework should be used flexibly.

Each type of discussion has advantages and disadvantages and presents the possibility either for good use or for abuse. The purpose of the model is to clarify the choices available to the individual teacher in order to improve student speaking and listening capacities. Extensive observations of teachers validate the notion that many teachers view a discussion as the time for critical thinking, but, in truth, most identified discussions fall into the first quadrant. They are dominated by good-intentioned teacher talk. As one teacher explained to me after viewing a videotape of her discussion, "I'm such a nice person! Until I was observed, I didn't realize how I keep cutting the kids off with questions."

Conclusion

There is a general consensus that we need more high-level reasoning in our classrooms. Although some educators advocate teaching thinking skills as a separate subject, I side with those who believe critical and creative thinking must be integrated into the curriculum and into classroom life in order to have long-range validity.

Teachers in every discipline must embody the critical disposition. They must self-monitor so that their behavior is a reflective model for students. As teachers plan their sessions and write the word *discussion* in their plan books, they must be more aware of what the term means and genuinely plan to promote student thought.

All teachers, in every field and at every level of instruction, need to be deliberate in their efforts to encourage quality speech and quality listening in their classrooms. The Discussion Types Model is intended to sharpen these skills while providing a key cross-disciplinary literacy strategy. Both student and teacher can monitor the exchange of ideas and create even more powerful responses.

Teachers from every discipline can contribute to student success by using a formal approach to speaking skills through four discussion types that are assessable.

6

Tuning the Speaking/Listening Instrument

Giving Voice Lessons in Each Classroom

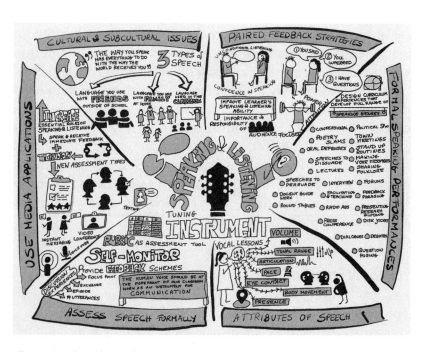

Illustration by Silvia Tolisano

In the world of school, speaking is our most immediate and consistently used language capacity. Through it we convey who we are and what we think. As educators, we rely squarely on our personal vocal capability to share, to influence, to empower, and to engage. Our field of practice is predicated on communicating through effective speaking and listening. Yet in terms of formal instructional focus, we tend to neglect these critical language capabilities with our students. This chapter dives into questions regarding fundamentals of speaking and listening. How can Johnny develop confidence and competence in the quality of his voice? How can Maria's teachers expand the range of her speaking opportunities? How can they give useful and nonthreatening feedback? How do we assist our learners to become genuine and attentive listeners?

Like a fingerprint, each human voice is totally unique. There is no ideal. Voices are colored by range, pitch, tone, texture, accent, and age, as are musical instruments. The voice reveals the emotional state of a person—the implicit feeling behind any set of words. And the words chosen by a person tell us about his or her culture, background, and whether or not the person wishes to fit in or stand apart from others in any given situation.

Good speakers rely on listening to make meaning from what they hear. In order to speak effectively, we must both listen to others and be able to hear ourselves. This process requires constant feedback. However, feedback on the way an individual speaks can become a sensitive issue because it involves another's perception of the speaker. Because such feedback can generate sensitive issues, especially with children, it is easy to avoid addressing them in the classroom.

Feedback From Siri

The opportunity for feedback using digital tools, media making, and global connectivity for speaking and listening is astounding. Siri, the voice activated and feedback function on the iPhone, immediately shows the speaker the level of volume. If the speaker is clear, Siri listens and provides an answer to the question or request (if it is within reason). The opportunity to provide students with personal and immediate feedback on their speech using digital tools is a gift to teachers. What is clear is that whether classical or contemporary in approach, there is an overarching need to ramp up speaking and listening in our literacy approach.

We spend an enormous amount of time and energy encouraging our students in the development of their writing abilities. In English class, we teach them the term *voice* to help them establish an authentic and personal style. Yet we are oddly negligent when addressing the identical questions in classroom speech. It is as if a teacher assumes a child is born with a voice that is not amenable to improvement without the benefit of a speech or drama coach. Classroom teachers need to recognize that the human voice is an individual instrument and that music teachers, drama coaches, and speech therapists can help them help their students to perfect it. Simultaneously, there is a corresponding need for accentuating listening responses.

As one of the nation's leaders on developing effective speaking skills in our schools, Eric Palmer (2011) notes:

> Imagine walking into a ninth grade English course to observe the teacher. As you enter, the teacher informs you that he will not be teaching writing this year because the students already know how to write. The teacher can prove this and show you the "what I did last summer" paragraph, emails, and text messages from online chat rooms. That seems absurd doesn't it? It is equally as absurd when you imagine a teacher saying this about speaking: "I will not be teaching speaking this year because my students already know how to speak." Students need direct instruction to help them speak effectively, just as they need direct instruction to help them write effectively.
>
> (p. 7)

The previous chapter on discussion types attempted to provide teachers with strategies to increase the quality of student interaction in group settings. This chapter recommends classroom practices that support strategies for increasing individual vocal capacity in every K–12 classroom:

1. Create and nurture speaking and listening partners in class in the spirit of writing process, paired feedback strategies.
2. Face and work with cultural and subcultural issues regarding grammar and syntax as opposed to ignoring them.
3. Employ and examine attributes of speech, and consider excellent models of oratory.
4. Design formal speaking performance assessments reflecting a range of genres.
5. Utilize media applications to record the voice and deliberately integrate into assessment designs.
6. In discussion events, assess speech as formally as writing is assessed.

Speaking and Listening Partners: Lessons From the Writing Process

One of the great contributions from the writing process work developed by Donald Graves (1983), Shelly Harwayne (1987), Lucy Calkins (1994), and Nancie Atwell (2002) is their emphasis on feedback. Trust is built between the reader and writer as they learn and practice in pairs. Precise supportive feedback is the goal. The writing process assists learners to identify, formulate, and provide high-quality feedback. Through the use of carefully constructed rubrics, role-playing and practice, learners (even our youngest learners) can become helpful readers to developing writers. Although there is no guarantee that every student will benefit from our instruction, certainly direct instruction from teacher to student is at the core of quality teaching of writing techniques. In addition to our direct instruction, however, student peer editing provides feedback that helps readers to focus on what is precise, useful, and supportive. Furthermore, the reader develops this same capability for his or her own writing. Everyone wins. I believe that, with some adaptation, this paradigm can improve a learner's speaking and listening abilities.

Children and adolescents are vulnerable. When they speak, they need to know that someone is fully listening. I suggest that classroom teachers periodically set up opportunities for students to gain control and power over their ability to speak by formally setting up carefully structured *unconditional listening sessions*. Working in pairs, one student shares a point of view or an experience with another student who listens thoughtfully *without interruption* for at least five full minutes. This activity may seem like some kind of miracle, but it is possible. The other student waits, listens intently, and responds directly by identifying what was said and what was inferred, and by raising any pertinent questions. Although a teacher must be discerning about the matching of these pairs, given the amount of paired work done in writing process workshops in our language arts and English classes, it is doable. The act of unconditional listening is a rarity, and it is a gift for a child or adolescent. Confidence in speaking can be coupled with unconditional listening. Consider the daily practice sessions conducted in any foreign language class. Even if the sessions are scripted in some instances, students do listen and speak in pairs.

The way we speak is affected by the way our audience listens. We can help our students in the development of their voices by making them aware of the audience. Years ago I had the opportunity to work with the New York City Ballet Education Department under the direction of Michele Audet, founding director, who developed a program called Storytelling through Dance. The dancers from the ballet worked with classroom teachers in the New York City and metropolitan areas to make ballet accessible and engaging. Students participated by identifying a range of audiences and the appropriate behaviors one would need to display. Students simulated the sounds and body language of the crowd at a New York Yankee game at Yankee Stadium, the behavior of a classroom when a teacher speaks, the audience at Lincoln Center where the New York City Ballet performs, and the audience that one becomes when intently listening to a friend.

It was a terrific activity that inspired students to reflect on situational listening. What was revealed, however, goes way beyond audience decorum. Michele's insight continues as a member of Terpsichore Quest, continuing to support these efforts in arts programs.

Students recognized the power of focused attention and the importance and responsibility of the audience. They could see how the speaker or performer interacts with the attentiveness of the audience or listener. As one child said, "There is a dance between the dancers and all of us in the seats."

Working Through Cultural and Subcultural Issues in Classroom Speech

Please read the following questions. Note that the answer to each question is "world language class."

- ◆ In which middle school or high school class do you hear each student talk every day?
- ◆ In which class do you hear students regularly speak aloud and interact with other students in a direct and formal way?
- ◆ In which class is there a consistent expectation of and instruction for clearly articulated language patterns?
- ◆ In which class do students accept and expect that the teacher will and should assist them with and insist on oral grammatical correctness?
- ◆ In which class is there open and regular group practice on pronunciation?

As noted earlier in this book, we turn again to instruction in a new language, a foreign language or world language, to best answer questions about promoting literacy. Ironically, we focus more on developing individual student capacity in world language classrooms than in those where English is the primary medium. Students understand that their foreign language teachers expect and encourage them to pronounce new words, and that they will be asked to do so correctly. Any reasonable foreign language teacher assists students to edit their speech for grammatical correctness. Students want no less from their teachers. But outside our foreign language classrooms we too often allow students to proceed through classes and school using English with startling shifts in the accuracy of grammatical usage in speech. This practice is not supported or tolerated in a world language class. If it is acceptable in the subculture of the classroom, then there is a form of collusion that ultimately disables the language capacity of Rachel, Abdul, Johnny, and Maria. It is a sensitive issue. Teachers certainly do not want to demean or judge a child, especially in front of his or her peers; yet we do not want to ignore habits that ultimately work against our learners. The following experience might prove helpful as we consider this dilemma.

Years ago I worked with teachers from an island in the Caribbean. A wonderful, warm teacher in the workshop made a striking statement about the way she runs her class regarding language. This is what she says to her classes:

> Students, when it comes to speech, there are basically three types of speech. One is the language you use with your friends out of school. Frankly, the way you use language with your friends is your business, just as it is mine with my friends. The next type is the language that you use at home with your family. This is private language, too, and you are never to correct your parents or another family member unless they request it. Finally, there is the language used in this classroom. In our class, we will use the Queen's English. Proper speech and grammar are supported. I want to give you power, and I want to give you choices. The way you speak has everything to do with the way the world will receive you.

This teacher raises the issues of culture and subcultures that influence a child's life. She is realistic and respectful with her students. Her goal is confidence building. She knows that we are weakened when we do not have the ability to select and revise our speech to adapt to various environments. We can easily envision a student who raises his or her hand to ask a question or to make a comment. When the comment or question has an obvious grammatical error, and when others snicker or even openly laugh, often the student does not know why. Otherwise, the student would have used the appropriate grammar to begin with. In short, common sense tells us that many students do not actively participate in class because they have had embarrassing moments. A school culture should provide an ongoing support structure that fuels students with a desire to take risks, whether they are kicking a pass on the soccer field or adding to a discussion in a science class.

Attributes of Speech: Vocal Lessons in Each Class

Let's try another scenario. In what classes are you likely to hear the most attention given to projection, enunciation, inflection, and feeling through the voice? Obvious answers are musical performance classes, speech classes, and drama classes. In these classes both learners and teachers assume that particular care and attention will be given to the voice as an instrument. Students often focus on breathing to provide more range to their voices and to keep the very muscles that control speech or singing relaxed. These classrooms give students the opportunity to gain confidence and to control their voices.

Teachers across the disciplines can coach their learners and elevate characteristics of speech using the same strategies as their speech and music colleagues down the hall. They can enable learners to raise their speech to a higher level of prominence in the classroom. With the growing number of language learners in our classrooms, as well as second language teachers, the need for more polished and precise speech should be front and center in instruction. Listed below are some attributes of voice with descriptions, suggestions, and key target questions for examination in the classroom. These attributes do not imply that all students should speak the same way; they simply help students become conscious of the use of these characteristics in their speaking choices. Any teacher in any subject can focus on these attributes as part of instruction. The target questions are hooks to engage students at any age to stop and consider how to "play their vocal instrument."

◆ **Volume:** *How can I turn up or turn down the volume to assist in my communication?* The degree of softness or loudness that is most effective should be determined formally. Not all students perceive the need for appropriate vocal volume in social and formal situations. On a more subtle level, a fascinating question that students can discuss is when altering volume within a speaking utterance assists communication.

◆ **Tonal range:** *When does a high or low pitch and inflection assist in communication? What is my range as a speaker? Can I increase my tonal range?* By extending the range of tones, a speaker has a greater vocal menu from which to choose when communicating. A classic monotone speech is, in fact, monotonous. In a sense, a student can think of tone as a musician thinks of pitch. There is no one ideal musical composition, but effective composers select the range of pitches and tones that best serve the musical message.

◆ **Articulation:** *How can I articulate my words so that others can follow precisely what I am trying to express?* Clarity of sound patterns at the beginning and ending of sounds is always emphasized when learning a new language. We should support this emphasis all the way through grade 12, as opposed to making it the focus only in the primary grades or in foreign language classes. Group pronunciation aloud of different terms in the content areas can become an integral part of introducing more complex types of terms.

◆ **Pace:** *How does the pace of my speech affect my listeners or audience? How can I use pace to present my ideas more effectively?* Speed of speech is a critical variable when addressing different audiences. Variations in speed serve different purposes. Students can reflect on their personal natural speed based on their family and cultural speech patterns. As individuals, learners can examine the pace of speech in a way that is natural and supportive of communication.

◆ **Eye contact:** *How can I have natural eye contact with people when I speak?* Natural eye contact should be comfortable for the speaker and the listener(s). Different types of speaking situations demand different levels of eye-contact intensity. Staring directly into a listener's eyes with a riveting glare is not necessarily the best way to present ideas. Looking away into space on a regular basis also distracts listeners from the speaker's message. When examining this attribute, students should look at a range of speaking situations, from an informal gathering of friends in a hallway to a formal sharing of materials to a class during a project.

◆ **Body movement:** *How can I use my body to support my communication in a way that feels natural to me?* Given student variables such as gender, culture, family, and physiology, we need to encourage a natural flow of body movement to support the communication skills of individual speakers. There are real cultural implications because children are raised in families and places with distinctive views of the body. Some children gesticulate aggressively when they speak, and it works for them because it is ingrained. Other children are more self-contained. The real classroom challenge is to work with children so that they are not stiff and uncomfortable with their bodies when they speak. In addition, if body movement is distracting, the message of the speaker is lost.

◆ **Presence:** *What is presence?* Speaking power is not only about command of the nuance of the instrument or the ability to dramatize or to make effect; it also has to do with commitment and intent. Students should identify the type of presence required of a professional actor or singer and contrast how that differs from the presence required of a teacher.

Engaging students in active identification of those traits that will improve their speech, and then having them practice those traits in an active learning environment are direct methods for improving student performance. The ability to find appropriate words in spoken interactions is central to every subject. If Johnny cannot say what he needs help with, he will struggle.

Just as we provide role models and examples of excellence in any performance or skill area that we are developing, we should encourage students to identify people who provide models of excellence for each of these vocal traits. Students should listen to segments of great oratory available to them from the past and from the present. If the visual presence of the person is available on film, video, or digital computerized images, I recommend that students listen first and then actually view the speaker. For example, we can listen first to Martin Luther King's "I Have a Dream" speech as a great example of pace, inflection, and presence through the speaking voice. When we later see the passion in his face, we can shift our focus to his eye contact and body language. Our learners need to "study" speaking and listening formally and with care and vitality.

Designing Formal Speaking Assessment Types

Most teachers can readily identify a range of writing assessment types represented in both fiction and nonfiction. Whether the subject is haiku poetry or a letter to the editor, teachers are accustomed to assigning writing tasks that match the ongoing learning experience in the classroom. It is usually more difficult to promote and assess the spoken word. In order to promote a spectrum of speaking opportunities, we can design curriculum experiences that develop the full range of speaking genres. It is fruitful to brainstorm a range of speaking assessments that respond to the question: What forms of speech do professionals in our field employ? For example, what types of formal speech are necessary to scientists? The responses may range from presenting findings at a symposium to questioning those same findings. The following is a list designed to instigate such a session:

confessional	phone calls
podcast host	poetry slams
debates	political spin
dialogues	presenting research findings
disc jockey	press conference
discussion groups	question posing
docent guide work	radio ads
facilitating and teaching	round tables
feedback phrasing	satire via fake news report
forums	sharing folklore
interviews	speeches to persuade
joke telling	speeches to dissuade
lectures	stand-up routine at a comedy club
making voice messages	therapy session
oral defenses	town meetings
paraphrasing	work-related situations

A wonderful opportunity emerges for educators to formally design speaking assessment benchmarks that fully explore a range of speaking genres among learners, much in the same way that we assess writing. In fact, any examination of state standards shows an overwhelming dominance of suggested writing assessments vs. formal speaking assessments. It is understandable that writing is the more common mode of assessment in academic work, yet there is a real problem here. Can one imagine a foreign language teacher avoiding formal feedback and evaluation of speaking and discussion skills on a regular basis?

A Gift to Teaching Speaking and Listening: Media-Making Tools

One of the great gifts of modern technology is the advent of new assessment types. For instance, we see students blogging and using IM-messaging to communicate with a certain fluidity and openness. Although leaders may be disturbed or distrustful of the abbreviations and lack of formality, it is a spontaneous, informal modality that encourages speech.

Video conferencing and webcasts allow students (as well as educators) to meet in virtual space and to communicate openly. I was thrilled to hear about a French teacher who was going to have her final oral examination for her highest-level students presented via a video conference with a school in France. In this way, her students could communicate in real time with students in France. They could time travel even as they sharpened their speaking and listening strategies.

New pocket-sized technologies that incorporate the easy reach of a cell phone with the visual image of the speaker need to be rethought for potential classroom use. Encouraging students to create documentary soundtracks with a voice-over is a marvelous way to introduce thoughtful examination of how phrasing and inflection are critical to a documentary. I believe that our 21st-century tools can expand our classroom communities and directly increase the essential roles of speaking and listening.

Concentrating on the integration of digital media applications provides an exceptional opportunity to encourage learners to speak and receive immediate feedback, often in conjunction with a visual project. Examples of these tools are Voice Thread (http://voicethread.com), Storybird (http://storybird.com), and Get-Puppet (http://get-puppet.co). A teacher can upgrade formative and summative assessments by using these tools in lieu of simply a writing piece.

Formal Feedback for Speaking

In terms of feedback on our vocal attributes, a rubric can provide another relatively objective means of providing useful assessment. The rubric can include the attributes presented in this chapter as well as criteria reflecting the proper use of speech. This parallels the type of rubric used in giving effective feedback for writing. An example of a speaking rubric is at www.read-writethink.org/files/resources/printouts/30700_rubric.pdf.

By using a rubric as an assessment tool, Johnny can learn to self-monitor and comment on how he is developing his pace or volume in the same way that he monitors the improvement of his writing.

If we develop a more formal speaking genre and emphasize more effective listening strategies, we need to provide more feedback schemes as well. During discussion experiences we can give students relatively objective feedback by identifying the following attributes of discussion:

- ◆ **Focus point:** The key premise, argument, or idea being shared
- ◆ **Exchange:** Each time a point is commented on by another group member
- ◆ **Episode:** When a series of at least three exchanges maintains focus on a key point
- ◆ **Number of utterances:** The "chit" marks received by each member in the group when he or she participates in the discussion

The goal in a discussion is for all members to participate, with a low number of episodes and with many exchanges. The achievement of this goal indicates that a point was developed more deeply than if there were no exchanges and few episodes, which would apply more to the recitation of a monologue than to a discussion.

When we acquire language, we begin as listeners, then speakers, then writers (as we make marks as children), and then readers. In order to raise the language capacity of our learners, we need to raise all of these aspects of language development in concert in our classrooms. The human voice should be in the forefront of our classroom work as an instrument for communication. Successful development of student voice requires thoughtful nurturance and care.

Teachers from every discipline can contribute to their students' development of poise, confidence, and power by employing direct technical instruction that promotes the use of the human voice and body as a speaking and communication instrument.

7

Activating Literacy in Our Plans

Upgrading Curriculum Maps K–12

Illustration by Silvia Tolisano

Best practices. These two words suggest the deliberate selection of our most refined and successful strategies based concretely on our work with children. In our field we never hear these phrases: "pretty good practices," "okay practices," or "leave-me-alone practices." Obviously, we want to be discerning about curriculum and instruction in the classroom and in that spirit I suggest there is an additional adjective and a noun to embrace: *current* practices and *possibilities.* How can we deliberately and effectively embed classical and contemporary literacies strategies into curriculum, assessment, and instruction? Curriculum Mapping is central to bringing the best of current practice and possibilities into classroom life.

If we want students to carry literacy strategies from classroom to classroom and subject to subject over time, then teachers can review their curriculum maps vertically and across grade levels, within and between disciplines. If we want our learners to demonstrate precise and consistent approaches to self-assessing their work, then the instructional skills we teach should be precise and consistently supported. If we want to see our students take risks in their work and demonstrate variety in what they produce, then our curricular and instructional practices should display a range of imaginative and timely assignments. We need to take imaginative and reasonable risks in our work. A key issue, then, is how we motivate and engage our professional staff in the process of implementing these active literacy approaches.

Professional development practices to assist teachers in building active literacy should reflect the rich and engaged types of experiences that we desire for our learners. Staff development is successful when there are corresponding successes in our students' work; in fact, it is the only way we concretely know that we are effective. If we wish to see performance improvements in our learners in sustained and cumulative growth over years, then we must recognize that capacity-building takes time and requires real continuity. The work in both classical and contemporary literacy needs to be mapped out and embedded in our curriculum and assessment designs over time.

Our efforts to both increase classical and new literacies are certainly well intended, but too often the follow up is informal and isolated. It is understandable that energy is put into a patchwork of workshops to address literacy problems and to encourage possibilities. Frequently, the strategies presented are susceptible to cherry picking by participants who scurry back to their classroom desks, covering them with scattered plans for the next day. The same can hold true for digital learning workshops but in a slightly different variation, given that a teacher can engage in a professional development experience and move on to finding exciting applications in isolation.

Committees work hard to create literacy documents to help teachers—documents that far too often find their way into a lost pdf file or even lost in a Google doc. Given the demands of the school day, a well-intended, even well-designed, workshop on literacy is not enough. We need a formal commitment both vertically Pre-K to grade 12 and across grade levels that is shared in common curriculum documentation.

Curriculum Mapping as a Collegial Commitment to Active Literacy

I believe that we need a genuine increase in *formality* in our work in every classroom: formal review of assessment data, demographic data, and curricular data among all teachers in targeted groups. This notion of formality differs from conversation and discussions that occur openly in ongoing meetings or informal interactions, as valuable as they may be. How do we get teachers to speak to one another in formal diagnostic discussion? How can we develop a vital curriculum to respond to the needs of our learners and formally monitor its development? How can we review and update that responsive curriculum in a formal and ongoing rigorous review process?

Consider the following reality. Johnny has a flotilla of teachers: six grade-level teachers plus at least four special-area teachers (art, music, physical education, and library) in elementary school. He probably will go on to his middle school and have approximately eight teachers per year in grades six through eight. In high school, given some semester-based courses, he will likely deal with around ten teachers per year. The total number of teachers that Johnny has over his thirteen years from K–12 ranges between forty and sixty-five.

Curriculum Mapping does not guarantee that all of these teachers will become intimately acquainted with Johnny's needs or his experience. What it can do is provide a real data base. Allowing any of his teachers to find out what he has experienced and is experiencing currently, and it can communicate with more precision with any of that flotilla of teachers through technology. By logging onto mapping software, a sixth grade social studies teacher, Ms. Goodwin, examines lasts year's fifth grade curriculum map from the feeder schools that sent their students to the receiving middle school. She can see what adjustments she might make to build on previous work. If there is a lack of clarity or a disparity, she can request the needed information via e-mail.

Deliberate Upgrading on Curriculum Plans

What is more, Ms. Goodwin can deliberately *upgrade* the map to ensure that the maps are activated for literacy with both classical strategies and digital tools. Consider the methods from Figure 7.1: Ms. Goodwin's American Revolution unit map has been upgraded to include a classical strategy to focus on revising the text to include more descriptive and vivid adjectives and a digital application, Visuwords, to assist the learner in the task. What is more, she is upgrading to have them use Voicethread to create a media recording to accompany the images in their project. Thus, the learners will get feedback on the cultivation of their speaking strategies.

This chapter does not purport to lay out the detailed model and specifics of instituting a full-scale mapping program, but rather attempts to show how the deliberate and strategic inclusion of literacy integration needs to be part of formal curriculum planning.

What Is Curriculum Mapping?

For over twenty years, work on Curriculum Mapping has proved to be a fruitful venue for helping teachers within and between buildings to improve student performance. Curriculum Mapping (Jacobs, 1997, 2004, 2012) allows teachers to critically examine what is actually going on in classrooms, both horizontally and vertically. By dealing with the reality of operational curriculum vs. proposed generic guidelines, teachers can make better decisions about how to adapt and revise the curriculum in order to accommodate and to extend Johnny's evolving skills.

Because of the array of software platforms supporting mapping, there is an immediacy to this approach that was simply not possible for previous generations of teachers. In this way it is clearly a 21st-century approach to the age-old problem of articulation and alignment. Curriculum Mapping is formal work. Individual teachers and teams of teachers create maps, and all teachers in a building or district can review each other's maps. Tens of thousands of schools are mapping throughout the world given Internet access, with the development of an increasing range of more sophisticated software versions.

Embedding both classical and new literacy proficiencies to be developed directly in curriculum maps is central to cultivating a collaborative culture that ensures a commitment to the strategies set out in this book.

Mapping: A Coin with Two Sides

Curriculum Mapping is a coin with two sides: one side is the actual documentation of the maps, which is best done electronically; the other side is the formal review process of those maps. The model that I have developed for Curriculum Mapping is a seven-phase data collection, analysis, and development procedure. The power of the model is its employment of *technology as a key communication device*. Through the use of a district Web site, a teacher can log on to an Internet site that stores the ongoing information about what is actually being taught at any point in the school calendar year. Because of the dynamic possibilities of technology, teachers can click on the assessment entries for their units and courses and store student work and records about the performance of individual learners. Mapping is being used in every state in the United States and throughout the world. The leading commercial mapping software groups and nonprofit education organizations have created programs that are easy to use and powerful tools that make mapping possible.

Clearly, any school wishing to develop academic power tools needs teachers across the curriculum to collaborate with each other to build consistency in reading, writing, speaking, and listening strategies.

Maps are shared by the professionals in a building and serve as a vehicle for better decision-making. Without this vehicle it is difficult to know in a public forum what, how, and when skills are being developed. Of equal importance, the skills are nested in the context of the content and are focused on essential questions, with a designated form that the assessment will take. In other words, if a teacher wishes to work on speaking and listening through the skill of interviewing, the map provides an opportunity to look for the most relevant and fruitful place in the course of the school year to work on that skill. Perhaps the teacher has elected to work on interviewing skills when teaching a unit on immigration. By encouraging students to interview immigrants to the United States with key essential questions in hand, the teachers have a resulting ready-made assessment in the form of a transcript. The transcript provides evidence that the student is acquiring knowledge about the reasons people immigrate; it also indicates the progress the student is making on interviewing strategies. Thus, the map is aligned. There is a genuine and viable line that logically connects the content, the skill, and the assessment. In addition, if the designated skills correspond directly to state, district, provincial, or national standards, then the map is further aligned.

Like so many education initiatives, language strategies across the curriculum will remain an isolated choice on the part of an individual teacher. Certainly, Johnny will benefit from a teacher who thoughtfully examines his or her own work over the course of a year to build the language competency of students. We would want no less from any professional. The problem is that Johnny has more than that one teacher, and there is a deep and pervading need for Johnny's teachers to speak and listen to each other, read each other's maps, and write revisions to help his progress along the way. We need to be readers, writers, speakers, and listeners with Johnny and his classmates. We need a formal collaborative model to make that happen. In fact, the inspiration for this book was revealed in a workshop in a public middle school grappling with this challenge.

A Revealing Middle School Vignette

My first revelations about the need for including literacy strategies came as a result of a frustrating dialogue among teachers in a well-regarded middle school with a range of student abilities in highly competitive Westchester County, NY, a suburb of New York City. Pressure was on each of these teachers because of the genuine demands of New York State's testing, which required extensive writing and very difficult reading prompts in every subject. We were attempting to begin Curriculum Mapping. The science teacher, who had been quiet through most of our session, suddenly expressed what everyone was feeling:

> How can we map our science program when we all know that a good-sized chunk of our students cannot even read or write with any genuine skill? Mapping is just making it clear that we can teach all we want, but the real skills these kids need are reading and writing. I keep getting science labs that I can barely follow these days. Sure, we have a lot of high-performing kids. We all know that, but let's get real. There are more and more kids coming to us from a couple of elementary schools without the basics.

The emotional wave that followed was intense and powerful. The focus of our work had been on mapping the curriculum and integrating the state standards in each subject. Yet when we began to examine the reality, the operational curriculum needed to assist a significant number of students was in fundamental literacy. It was evident that the second level of work was clearly cross-disciplinary and language based.

After all members of the faculty had voiced their concerns, the conversation continued to move toward blame. The blame centered primarily on the elementary schools that were part of the feeder pattern of students and on the English Department. This latter shift was not well received given that there were members of the English Department present in the room. It was apparent that many teachers thought it was the job of the English Department to help students improve in language arts and communication skills. "I teach science; I don't teach English" was the more common refrain. The chairperson of the English Department took offense and argued that the biggest problem was that each of the teachers had radically different standards and the students knew it:

> What is really being modeled here is inconsistency. If we keep pointing fingers at each other and one person cares about grammar while another one doesn't, then, of course, we are going to have kids all over the place.

The science teacher who had opened things up in the first place countered, "Okay, but you people in the English Department don't even agree on standards. The kids all know that, too!"

The meeting was heated, yet it was cathartic. Everyone cared. The blame game ended quickly. These were professional educators who without exception cared deeply about their students and about their craft. After about an hour we came to the conclusion that we would start mapping literacy. The English Department agreed to meet with each department and begin to work through some common and formal targets. Curriculum Mapping was the tool we used to address this problem, and it was this difficult and productive meeting that propelled my work into active literacy.

A Planning Model for Cross-Classroom Literacy Integration

The following model for mapping procedures has been featured in my books on mapping over the years (Jacobs, 1997, 2004, 2012), but is described with specific attention to both the focus on integrating classical literacy and contemporary literacies raised in this book:

♦ Phase 1: Make the case with student work through bi-level analysis.

♦ Phase 2: Identify essential cross-curricular language skills and contemporary literacies needing development K–12.

♦ Phase 3: Revise curriculum maps and corresponding lesson plans to improve student products/performance using identified strategies.

♦ Phase 4: Define and develop highly specific benchmark assessments on maps formally addressing targeted language skills and standards and contemporary literacies.

♦ Phase 5: Examine student assessments resulting from benchmarks for feedback to students and teachers vertically and horizontally.

♦ Phase 6: Feed analysis back into maps and each classroom to continue the spiral.

♦ Phase 7: All buildings in a common feeder pattern share findings K–12 in order to sustain and support the students in their transitions between buildings. This work is handled at building level, site-based curriculum councils and district level cabinets.

Phase 1: Making the Case With Student Work Through Bi-Level Analysis

A direct and powerful means of bringing faculty members to the table is through the most revealing evidence of learning: student work. In general, it is not difficult to find reasons for working on improving student performance. The key is to emphasize the need for *cumulative attention*. Carl Glickman (1993), in his compelling work with the League of Professional Schools in Georgia, suggests that a shared commitment to teaching and learning should become a *public covenant*. The curriculum map is a document reflecting this covenant. Teachers display for review the operational curriculum so that adjustments and revisions can be made over time. The focus is directly on the products and performances of learners.

In this initial prologue phase, a critical point of staff development should be based on the premise raised throughout this book; that is, each of the professionals in a building is a teacher of reading, writing, speaking, and listening. Chapter one raised arguments to support this contention, and it is of value to raise these points in the initial phase. For example, the argument that "it is the job of the English teacher" or "I don't have time to focus on these skills" is sometimes raised. Clearly, we are wasting students' time if they do not understand what they are listening to, if they cannot interact with what they are reading, if they give limited oral responses in class, and if there are vast inconsistencies in their writing. The English and language arts portion of a student's day is a kind of "boot camp" for language development and grammar. The English teachers are specialists, and in elementary education the language arts curriculum is the ultimate foundation of all language learning. However, it is the very isolation of this learning that prevents students from developing cumulative, consistent, and internalized language skills. It is unquestionably in Johnny's best interest for each and every teacher to make adjustments and to elevate the role of cross-disciplinary language skills in his or her classroom. Let us reverse this point. Can a case be made that it is in Maria's best interest *not* to make revisions and work towards cross-disciplinary skills cumulatively?

The most direct method for prompting school-wide commitment to Curriculum Mapping literacy strategies is to go straight to assessment pressure points. Teachers in a building might feel particularly "beholden" to the state test that looms in the spring. Bi-level analysis of specific sample test items on that examination, which are almost always available through state education Web sites, is a winning strategy for making the case. An elementary faculty could look at a specific math item designated for third grade on two levels of analysis: first, the math concept being tested, and second, the discrete reading and writing strategies requisite to carry out the work. The same analysis could occur with an advanced placement chemistry exam question among high school faculty. When educators literally stop and consider the precise combined set of subject-specific skills necessary for successful responses to a state examination at the same time that they look at the reading, writing, speaking, and listening skills that are necessary for the student to even approach the test, the case for school-wide collaboration is on the table. Bi-level analysis not only makes the case for mapping, but also readies a faculty to make precise and powerful responses on their maps.

We add now the dimension of examining student work presented in contemporary forms to see if there is a need for a more formal development of digital, media, or global competence. If, for example, a fourth grade teacher has asked students to share their work in environmental science on eco-systems in a Prezi (http://prezi.com) and the quality appears superficial, there may need to be a look at the requisite skills necessary to shape a more dynamic media presentation, although the content itself is current and relevant. It is looking at *two* levels of examination formally, whether classical or contemporary, that raises the bar for dynamic Curriculum Mapping.

Phase 2: Identifying Key Classical and Contemporary Literacy Strategies: Grades K–12 and Across Disciplines

If the root of all performance is based on student language facility, then a corresponding response from classroom teachers should be based on a thorough analysis of performance data to diagnose specific language needs. If a basis for being career and college ready requires students to be digitally literate, media savvy, and globally connected, then a corresponding analysis of these corresponding skills are in order. Data is needed. A data-driven curriculum is more than an intriguing notion; it is the only cumulative way to address the development of the very skills Johnny needs. What data should be examined? All student performances, whether standardized, criterion-based portfolio collections, traditional classroom quizzes, tests, media products, or long-term-project-based experiences, provide potentially useful information about our learners. The problem arises when data are viewed superficially, such as when test scores for a school district are posted in the local newspaper or a student receives a score of 40 on a test worth 100 points without the opportunity to find out specifically what skills are lacking. Analysis of mere numbers, however, can be helpful in determining which ones are individual flunks and which ones reflect long-term patterns needing long-term attention. When students are struggling, educators need access to two critical sets of information:

1. The original test or task with a breakdown of the items missed or the criteria that was lacking.
2. Analysis of those problem areas that distinguishes the precise skills that need development to assist learners, whether classical or contemporary.

Consider the medical doctor who is given information about a patient that simply states a number, the patient's temperature. Diagnosis requires highly discrete analysis of why the temperature is so high; it may take into account such factors as blood count, appetite, dizziness, muscle aches, possible bacterial infection, viral infection, recent travel experiences, current medications, and so forth. A proper prescription to lower the temperature is based on specific and thorough diagnostic information. The doctor relies on data reported by previous physicians and nurses. Treatment is cumulative. Furthermore, the doctor does not do the whole job of curing the patient. The doctor diagnoses the illness and prescribes treatment. Then it is up to the patient to follow the prescription faithfully. If the patient is unclear about the actions he or she must take and there are mixed messages from the team of doctors and nurses, the likelihood of healing diminishes.

In the same spirit, if we isolate a teacher with a reported score or with a portfolio of student work, there is a remarkably limited set of options for prescription. A teacher is likely to pummel the student inadvertently with more of the same; consequently, very little happens to improve conditions. In a school district in the south where I once worked, math scores were uneven on an eighth grade level state test. The faculty took the test apart and identified the root reason: students fell apart on word problems with long clauses and multiple tasks. They observed that nowhere in the math curriculum maps was special attention given to those specific paraphrasing tasks that would assist learners. I have often heard teachers report that students who do know a math concept may have so little reading practice that they fall apart in testing situations. In a powerful policy brief issued by the National Council of Teachers of English (2014), it is noted that:

> Student learning is also limited by testing's inflexible sorting of students into categories of proficient or not proficient. It can be very difficult for students designated as not-proficient to imagine themselves as effective readers and writers. This test-generated binary is troubling because it gives no space to the full range of features that comprise effective reading and writing. Students who have literacy abilities that extend beyond but do not fully encompass the narrow band of skills measured by standardized tests may not understand or appreciate their own capacities and become disengaged from school.

The integration of essential literacy strategies requires formality. There is a need for formal, precise alterations in the curriculum that reflect a K–12 perspective The individual teacher may be tempted, after reading about a technique or instructional tool, to run back to the classroom and use it there. But with active literacy that approach will not be sufficient. A group of teachers may read a set of literacy benchmarks and standards in language arts, comment on them, and see them as a kind of state-sanctioned checklist, but that will not be enough either. Our informality about examining and responding to data is a danger to learning because it leads us to believe we are making progress simply by going to meetings and talking about what our learners need.

Curriculum Mapping is formal work. It requires that teachers examine the electronic database of information entered by individual teachers about what they actually taught in a school year. With the operational curriculum anchored in real time, educators have an opportunity to make formal revisions. They can distribute the essential strategies among the professional public in a school and view them deliberately and openly. Instead of retreating into the classroom, the faculty can analyze gaps that need addressing collectively and cumulatively. Two sets of glaring gaps have been addressed in these pages: the dearth of formal literacy strategies in each class and the need for specific approaches to integrate new formats for learning given our digital and media possibilities.

Phase 3: Revise Curriculum Maps and Improve Student Performance Cumulatively

Revision allows us to "see again." The act of revision is an opportunity to return to an initial effort and to make a purposeful change that reflects what we have learned. Recently a curriculum director from Texas reinforced this point when she said, "I am thrilled these days because our teachers K–12 are finally reviewing maps together, making needed adjustments and our *curriculum is breathing*." Ultimately, we hope that the revision will improve the next round of curriculum development and instructional delivery. When we revise our maps, we can identify critical cross-disciplinary skills, enter them into our curriculum maps, and align them with corresponding literacy-rich products and performances with an eye to contemporary possibilities. A good practice during the revision stages is to strive for more specific assessment types. When our curriculum designs have broad and generic assessment types, we tend to obtain results from our learners that are broad, generic, and even clichéd. Revision of maps for stronger and modern types of responses leads to more sophisticated and engaged responses from our learners.

For example, if a high school science teacher wants to teach students how to make clear and articulate observations in a report, he or she may have better results if the generic word "report" is changed to a more specific request, such as "grant proposal or video documentary." Or if a fourth grade teacher asks students to write a paragraph in social studies about their community, he or she probably will have more success if the assignment is revised to a more specific request, such as "case study shared on a webpage," as if the children were modern-day anthropologists. Specificity breeds focus and emphasis on form to best serve the specific purpose and function of the writing.

A key practice discussed is the development of consensus maps (Jacobs, 2004, 2012). In this way there can be agreement among faculty about the types of genres that Rachel will encounter over the years and when she will be introduced to them. Thus we can avoid the unnecessary repetition that occurs when teacher after teacher introduces "historical fiction" or "free verse." We want to be sure that our learners are introduced to writers from a full range of genres and, in turn, that our students also have the opportunity to express themselves through a full range of genres. In each discipline educators should work together vertically K–12 to identify the point at which students should be exposed to the types of work that professionals in the field produce.

Phase 4: Mapping Benchmark Assessment Tasks That Address Targeted Literacy Skills

One of the hallmarks of an effective school is collaboration among the entire faculty to monitor and analyze student performance. It is genuine accountability when the faculty and administrators do not wait for a state or national test to "ambush" the learners, but take responsibility for their learners instead. With Curriculum Mapping, this process is not only doable, but also the core of its promise. After teachers have reviewed the maps vertically between grade levels and horizontally across subjects for a seamless integration of content, skills, and assessment, they are ready to formally co-design performance tasks, review portfolios (traditional or digital), or create constructed or selective response tests based on the specific areas needing attention for their particular student population. These common tasks are internally designed benchmark assessments, as opposed to externally designed assessments from organizations ranging from state education departments to the ACT, SAT, and the College Board. In short, they are locally designed benchmark assessments that have a purpose and a curricular context. To assist in the planning and designing of modern-day assessments, Figure 7.1 provides some examples that I have compiled to show how specific types of assessments can instigate dynamic responses. Key is the focus on career competence

Upgraded Assessment Types

3-D Modeling/Printing/ Scanning	Film study/critique	Programming/Coding
Animation	Forecasting/Projecting/	Project Planning Tool
Blogging/Forum	Global Forums virtual	Prototypes
Broadcasting channel	Graphics/Image	Researching/VettingTools
Case Studies on Website	Graphics Organizer	RSS Feeding
Collaborating	Graphing	Screencasting
Database	Grant proposal	Screenplay
Data Visualizing &	Infographics	Sketch-noting with tools
Digital Audio/Podcast	Info-Database Searches	Spreadsheets analysis
Digital Game Creating	Interactive Simulation	Station hosting - podcast
Digital Storytelling	Internet Researching	Storyboarding
Digital Porfolio	Mashing/Remixing	Survey design
Digital Video	MathematicalModeling	Timeline interactive/virtual
Drawing	Media critiques	Video Hosting
E-Publication Creating	Music e-composition	Web Authoring/Curation
Entrepreneurial plan	Photo blogging	Webinar event hosting
Fact-checking repository (snopes.com)	Playlist - annotated	Word Processor
	Podcast - audio	Word Recognition
	Presentation - Prezi	Video/Image Synthesizing

H.H.Jacobs. *Active Literacy Across the Curriculum: Connecting Digital, Media, and Global Competence.* Routledge Pub. 2017.

FIGURE 7.1 Upgraded Assessment Types

and demonstration; for example, we might ask, "What does the modern day engineer produce? What does a contemporary historian create?"

When a school has collected the data concerning real-time information about the operational curriculum, there is a possibility for transformation. Teachers can sit together and insert specific revisions into existing maps and thus target specific cross-disciplinary language skills and contemporary literacy strategies. For example, in the course of a unit on Ancient civilizations, a social studies teacher can concentrate on editing for complete sentences concurrently with her emphasis on the development of observational skills

If the entire K–12 staff finds that students lack notetaking capabilities, they should organize a school-wide effort to focus on formal and deliberate benchmark assessments designed developmentally. A Notetaking Portfolio Benchmark can be entered on the maps at the end of the first ten weeks of school. Thus, notetaking strategies can be incorporated into lesson plans on the elementary school level. What is more, the benchmark can include sketchnoting using digital tools like Paper Fifty-Three. For example, teachers in grade three could introduce incremental developmental skills, from entering icons or words on jumbo cards to categorizing simple facts with a tool like Quizlet. The middle school and high school teachers might formally collect notes from students in a range of content areas to create a notetaking portfolio on Livebinder for examination. Teachers could then examine the notes to see if their efforts to increase student text interaction are succeeding. What the curriculum map does, in effect, is provide a specific time and basis for a school-wide focus on precisely what the learner needs and a means to assess how effectively teachers are adjusting curriculum and instruction to match those needs. The building benchmarks should appear on both the school or district consensus maps and the teacher's individual map.

Phase 5: Examining Student Benchmark Assessments Results to Provide Feedback to Students and Teachers

Upon completion of the benchmark assessment, teachers can view the results both vertically and horizontally in order to focus on the precise skill and/or content areas that need attention. The cycle continues as teachers revise their maps on the basis of the new information gained through the benchmark review process. If more attention to notetaking is needed, for example, then it is reinforced on each map.

Using bi-level analysis, a faculty should identify not only the subject matter concepts and skills needing attention, but also the gaps in language capabilities. For example, they might begin to identify both key terminology and high-frequency words that are proving problematic. Finding the editing and revision strategies that need critical attention in their curriculum designs, they can revise their own maps in conjunction with their colleagues.

TABLE 7.1 Native American Cultures: Anasazi, Makah, Mississippians

Teacher: Helen Krasnow (updated by H.H. Jacobs) *Subject: Grade 6 Social Studies* *Time frame: six weeks, November–December*

Unit: Native American Cultures: Anasazi, Makah, Mississippians

ESSENTIAL QUESTIONS	CONTENT	SKILLS	ASSESSMENTS
◆ How is culture affected by the environment? ◆ How does a group's culture affect the environment? ◆ Why are Native American legends important?	◆ CONCEPT: *Culture is a system of beliefs shared by a group.* ◆ Native American Case Studies: Relationship of Three Tribes to Specific Environments ◆ ANASAZI—PEOPLE OF THE DESERT ◆ MAKAH—PEOPLE OF THE COAST ◆ MISSISSIPPIANS—PEOPLE OF THE RIVER ◆ TERMS: mesa, potlach, artifact, culture, native, legend, ceremony, ritual	◆ Identify the differences and similarities among the Anasazi, the Makah, and the Mississippians. ◆ *Explain how the people in the different tribes express themselves through the arts and religious and spiritual practices.* ◆ Describe the time period during which each culture flourished. ◆ Identify Native American tribal locations on a geographical map of the United States. ◆ Create symbols to represent the cultures of the 4 different Native American tribes in this unit. ◆ **TRANSLATE directions on all assignments—high frequency words from list.** ◆ **EMPLOY all terms actively in writing and in speech.** ◆ EDIT for complete sentences on all formal work. ◆ **REVISE writing using more descriptive and vivid adjectives.**	◆ Class discussions in pairs **with report out notes on Class Blog** ◆ Chart of Native American traditions using ReadWriteThink. org ◆ Written response to focus questions on our Edmodo Class Site. ◆ Written assignment on a Native American legend ◆ Native American project on specific aspect of lifestyle ◆ Native American book report comparing two points of view ◆ **Accurate directions** ◆ **Correct and frequent use of terms in written work and orally** ◆ **Revisions marked in written work with** *inserted adjectives*

Phase 6: Feeding Analysis Back Into Maps for Each Classroom to Continue the Spiral

Teachers can turn to their maps collectively and make changes to their instructional designs based on the actual needs of their learners. In this way, *the entire faculty has, in fact, become a formal review team*. The spiral of growth continues as the faculty habituates the concept of reviewing student work on two levels of analysis.

The high school map presented in Table 7.2 shows entries from the calculus teacher that reflect not only the standards and needs of the learners in the mathematical components, but also the literacy strategies that were revealed as necessary through the examination of benchmark assessments. The teacher revised the map from its original projection in response to gaps revealed in benchmark assessments. In particular, notice that "Terms" appears as part of the content, as it should given that the terms do embrace key concepts requisite for carrying out the mathematical equations. The verbs are written in capital letters to serve as indicators of the actions to be taken by the learner. Then, in a turn to the modern, the teacher inserts a specific application, GeoGebra, to engage students with a digital interactive application that clearly visualizes the concept. This is formal intricate work.

Educators have long been confused about the reality gap between the "proposed itinerary" of standards and guidelines and the "real trip." Simply because a state standards says that Maria should be able to edit for complete sentences by the sixth grade does not ensure that this will be so. It is not to diminish the importance of setting a standard, just as there are markers for a travel plan. Mapping helps teachers to actualize the standards through examination of real-time data and revision on the basis of what students in a specific school system and grade level need. Mapping is both diagnostic and prescriptive because the key people who share the same students and the same building also share the same curricular journey.

The essential strategy proposed here is based on building a commitment to formal mapping of classical literacy, coupled with contemporary literacies, directly into curriculum plans. After years

TABLE 7.2 Sample of Revised Calculus Map

Content	Skills	Assessments
Essential Questions: 1. How is the equation of a line represented? 2. Why is the graph of a line different from the graph of a radical function? 3. Why is the graph of a line different from the graph of a rational function?	Rewrites linear equations in point slope form, slope intercept form, and standard form Determines slope of a line using slope formula Determines the equation of a line, given two points Creates a profit equation given fixed and variable costs Applies depreciation formulas Graphs functions on the T1–83+ calculator Determines the roots of rational and radical functions using calculations menu in the T1–83+ calculator	♦ Demonstration of slope employing GeoGebra ♦ TRIAD class discussions IN SMALL GROUPS REPORTING OUT TO WHOLE CLASS on linear functions ♦ Multiple choice quiz on slope and linear functions using WolframAlpha ♦ SHORT ANSWER test on functions and graphs via GeoGebra
Content: Linear functions Slope of a line ♦ Applications of linear functions ♦ Graphs of rational and radical functions Terms: Slope, function, depreciation, intercept, radical, rational	EMPLOYS terms in written work and in discussion TRANSLATES directions on all tests and assignments REVISES all written work to include precise procedural language EDITS all written work for complete sentences DISPLAYS evidence of linear functions visually	Correct use of terms in work Accurate paraphrasing of directions Circled revisions Edited written work GeoGebra response

of working with educators on Curriculum Mapping and examining entries on maps, I have found that there is clearly an undercurrent in our students' real journey. That undercurrent is literacy.

The standards chess move that has emerged from the design decision by CCSSO to integrate science, social studies, and technical subjects into the ELA standards was a genuine curricular "checkmate." No longer can academic subjects point to simply covering their content; it is critical that the modern learner communicate with language in all subjects. What is advocated here is that the deliberate integration of both classical and contemporary forms of communication is necessary in every subject in a formal approach demonstrated in assessments.

Mapping Reveals Reality Versus a Fantasy Curriculum

Those who rigidly follow the proposed itinerary without recognition of or adjustment for the literacy gap are using a fantasy curriculum that leaves many of our learners further and further behind. An examination of the disparity between *pacing guides* and revised updated and regularly reviewed maps shows the isolation of teachers and the lack of direct communication among professionals in a district and within each school. Decisions are made on an "as if" basis: as if Maria, Johnny, Rachel, and Abdul really have "traveled" to the places the guide says they have visited so that the next teacher can take them on a continuation of the tour. The truth is that perhaps Johnny did not go there. He might have moved slowly or he might have raced through the proposed and paced itinerary.

The Good Literacy News

When I wrote the first edition of this book I argued that we pulled the language rug right out from under our learners in fourth or fifth grade. After years of examining curriculum maps which reflect the actual documentation of the operational curriculum in calendar time, it was clear to me that formal literacy strategies were rarely taught after the fourth grade. Unless a child was formally declared "at risk," a horrible term suggesting a disease, all bets were off for remediation of literacy problems after fourth grade. That was then. The good news is that this perspective has changed with the press for more integration of classical literacy in all subjects at all levels of instruction, evidenced in the design of standards from Common Core to Next Generation Science to the National Social Studies Frameworks.

When it comes to curriculum guides and purchased programs, it is important to be aware that there is a real tendency to prepare them on an "as if" basis; as if Johnny is a fluent and competent reader by the time he reaches third grade. With mapping practitioners are encouraged to make adaptations based on the actual needs of the actual learners in a setting.

For example, texts, materials, and curriculum become increasingly dense and demanding with each passing year, relying on Johnny's language capacity to get him through seven or eight subjects competently. Adaptation is critical on a formal and collaborative basis between the teachers who share the same learners over time.

What is also clear after a reading of elementary school maps is that in some schools fierce turf wars rage over the whole- and part-language approaches. Johnny's real journey could take him from a "letter of the week" teacher in kindergarten to a whole-language teacher in first grade who uses "surface texts." His teachers can read, but he cannot. He is simply trying to *read* his teachers and what they want him to do. The last thing a student needs is a confusing sequence of vastly varied approaches to the foundations of reading, writing, speaking, and listening. Mapping is a virtual platform and review process where instructional pedagogy and approach to any subject can be worked out.

An examination of the maps of his secondary school teachers will reveal whether the assumption has been made that Johnny has the fundamental language equipment to handle the basic reading, writing, speaking, and listening required of him, or whether an emphasis on those very skills is integrated into units and lesson plans. It may be true that Mr. James, the math teacher, was trained to teach math to high school students, *not* to teach them to read math or to understand the words he uses at the blackboard. However, Mr. James is also capable of integrating necessary literacy competencies formally into his curriculum to ensure Johnny's understanding of mathematics. If produced with integrity, maps will reflect the reality.

Mapping is predicated on the need to reach every classroom, given the remarkable confluence of factors via computerized databases. We are well into the 21st century, and every field of practice in every profession shares information rapidly and dynamically. We need to do the same in education. Clearly the power to make meaningful revisions of curriculum plans and teaching strategies based on an open and shared platform is central to our ability to be responsive to our learners.

A critical and influential study in 2002 provided impetus to Curriculum Mapping. The Ohio State Educational Administration Association released the results of a study carried out by the Evaluation Unit at Indiana University. The study consisted of a range of variables related to student performance and looked at the top fifty performing schools. The first and most commonly cited factor contributing to sustained improvement is *Curriculum Mapping for alignment to standards*. The point is not simply matching with state standards, but aligning the curriculum among schools that share the same feeder pattern. One key to success is to make adjustments to the curriculum that align with what our students need in specific locations. The next factor is that professional development must focus not just on the earning of in-service credits (the pulse test), but also on the recognition that teacher growth is linked directly to student growth. The third factor is a *persistent and determined emphasis on literacy*, a factor that resonates directly with the premise made here. A fourth factor in the success of these schools is the use of ongoing tracking and monitoring of performance data that educators can use to determine what adjustments should be made in their current curriculum maps. The fifth factor is intervention and remediation for at-risk learners as soon as possible. Finally, test preparation strategies are developed so that learners feel more power in a range of testing situations. Key here is that these factors must be bundled. There is a need for formal, analytic, and persistent monitoring of student performance data that can be integrated directly in K–12 maps.

Phase 7: All Buildings in Common Feeder Patterns Sharing Findings K–12 to Sustain and Support Students in Their Transitions Between Buildings

Communication between buildings in a common feeder pattern within a district or campus is critical to success, and mapping makes it a natural next step. The formality of this approach to communication between educators in the chain of care for the learner ensures a method that supports accountability and monitoring. Larger school districts or large school campuses often create *consensus maps*, which replace guidelines as an agreed upon set of targets for the school to address. Just as the degree of detail on a GPS viewpoint of a specific geographic location can be an aerial view that is broad or a granular view on a specific street, the same is true with Curriculum Mapping. Consensus maps are wide-angle and big-picture views where agreements are made. This work is handled at building-level, site-based curriculum councils and district level cabinets.

Conclusion

The Curriculum Mapping review process is the seventh essential strategy for developing active literacy within our schools. Curriculum Mapping is a remarkable, technologically based vehicle for integrating the other strategies presented here. We need a common place to review and formally examine our concerns about learners, a place that is dynamic. Because we can go to our curriculum maps from any place given Internet access, we can readily find out precisely what is going on in our school in any classroom immediately. We can focus on varying the three types of vocabulary, editing and revision strategies, creative notetaking, discussion types models, or speaking skills opportunities. We can integrate digital tools and create media-making opportunities, and global connections. With mapping software platforms, there are new solutions and possibilities for school-wide engagement that did not exist before. To address the complex and difficult issues that literacy poses, we must fuse timeless practice with timely possibilities directly in each teacher's curriculum to guide every one of our students.

Imagine if every teacher across the grade levels entered similar entries on his or her maps no matter what the subject. Imagine if every teacher across grade levels formally entered best literacy practices with consistency and with an eye to the big picture of performance K–12. In this case, Johnny, Rachel, Abdul, and Maria would encounter a consistent focus on the language capacity strategies that are necessary for each of them to succeed both in school and beyond. With Curriculum Mapping software and programs all over the world, these worthy goals are not just for the imagination. Twenty-first-century tools are solving the age-old problem of making active literacy possible in every classroom K–12.

Teachers from every discipline can use Curriculum Mapping as a unifying school-wide vehicle to develop formal benchmark assessments to ensure active classical and contemporary literacy in every subject and for every grade level.

Bibliography

Atwell, Nancie. *Lessons that Change Writers*. Portsmouth, NH: Heinemann, 2002.

Barton, Mary Lee. Addressing the literacy crisis: Teaching reading in the content areas. *NASSP Bulletin*, Volume 81: 23, 1997.

Beck, Isabel L., McCoweon, Margaret G. and Kukan, Linda. *Bringing Words to Life*. New York, NY: Guilford Press. 2013.

Bellack, Arno. *The Language of the Classroom*. New York, NY: Teachers College Press, 1966.

Benjamin, Amy. *Writing in the Content Areas*, 2nd ed. Larchmont, NY: Eye on Education, 2005.

Benjamin, Amy, and Golub, Barbara. *Infusing Grammar into the Writers Workshop*. New York, NY: Routledge, 2016.

Biemiller, Andrew. *Language and Reading Success*. Brookline, MA: Brookline Books, 1998.

Billmeyer, Rachel. *Teaching Reading in the Content Areas*, 2nd ed. Denver, CO: MACREL, 1998.

Bloom, Benjamin. *Taxonomy of Educational Objectives: Cognitive Domain*. White Plains, NY: Longman, 1956.

Brookfield, Stephen and Peskill, Stephen. *Discussion as a Way of Teaching: Tools and Techniques for Democratic Classrooms*, 2nd ed. San Francisco, CA: Josey-Bass, 2005.

Calkins, Lucy. *Art of Teaching Writing*. Toronto: Irwin Publishing, 1994.

CCSSO (Council of Chief State School Officers). *Common Core State Standards* (retrieved from www.corestandards.org/).

Dillon, James T. Using questions to depress student thought. *The School Review* Volume 87, November, 1978.

Dillon, James T. *Questioning and Teaching*. New York, NY: Teachers College Press, 1988.

Donnelly, Tim. 9 brilliant inventions made by mistake. *Inc.com*, August 15, 2012 (retrieved from www.inc.com/tim-donnelly/brilliant-failures/9-inventions-made-by-mistake.html).

Evans, Thomas P. *Flanders System of Interaction Analysis and Science Teacher Effectiveness.* Paper presented at the annual NARST meeting, Minneapolis, Minnesota, March 8, 1970.

Glickman, Carl. *Renewing America's Schools: A Guide for School-Based Action.* Boston, MA: Jossey-Bass. 1993.

Graves, Donald. *Writing: Teachers & Children at Work.* Portsmouth, NH: Heinemann, 1983.

Harwayne, Shelley and Calkins, Lucy. *The Writing Workshop: A World of Difference.* Portsmouth, NH: Heinemann, 1987.

Hirsch, E.D. A wealth of words. The social order. *City-Journal.org.* Winter 2013 (retrieved from www.city-journal.org/html/wealth-words-13523.html).

Hyerle, David and Alper, Lawrence. *Student Successes with Thinking Maps.* Thousand Oaks, CA: Corwin, 2011.

Jackson, Tony and Boix-Mansilla, Veronica. *Educating for Global Competence: Preparing Our Youth to Engage the World.* New York and Washington, DC: Asia Society and CCSSO, 2011.

Jacobs, Heidi Hayes. *Mapping the Big Picture: Interdisciplinary Curriculum Design and Implementation.* Alexandria, VA: ASCD, 1997.

Jacobs, Heidi Hayes. *Getting Results with Curriculum Mapping.* Alexandria, VA: ASCD, 2004.

Jacobs, Heidi Hayes. *Curriculum 21: Essential Education for a Changing World.* Alexandria, VA: 2010.

Jacobs, Heidi Hayes. *Mapping to the Core: Integrating the CCSS into Your Local School Curriculum* (Lumibook). Salt Lake City, UT: SINET, 2012.

Jacobs, Heidi Hayes. Curricular intersections of the new literacies, in *Leading the New Literacies* (ed. H.H. Jacobs). Bloomington, IN: Solution-Tree, 2014.

Jacobs, Heidi Hayes and Alcock, Marie Hubley. *Bold Moves for Schools: How We Create Remarkable Learning Environments.* Alexandria, VA: ASCD, 2017.

Jacobs, Heidi Hayes and Baker, Frank W. Designing a film canon study and curriculum, in *Mastering Media Literacy* (ed. H.H. Jacobs). Bloomington, IN: Solution-Tree, 2014.

Palmer, Eric. *Well-Spoken: Teaching Speaking to All Students.* Portland, ME: Stenhouse Publishers, 2011.

National Commission on Writing in America's Schools and Colleges. *The Neglected "R": The Need for a Writing Revolution*. New York: The College Board, 2003.

National Center for Educational Statistics. *Performance of U.S. 15-Year-Old Students in Science, Reading, and Mathematics Literacy in an International Context. First Look at PISA 2015*. U.S. Department of Education (retrieved from https://nces.ed.gov/pubs2017/2017048.pdf).

National Council of Teachers of English. *Policy Brief: How Standardized Testing Shape and Limit Student Learning*. Urbana, IL: Author, 2014.

Schwartz, Katrina. Blogpost: *Making Learning Visible: Doodling Makes Memories Stick*, June 15, 2015.

Stall, Steven A. and Nagy, William E. *Teaching Word Meanings*. Mahwah, NJ: Lawrence Erlbaum, 2005.

Strong, Richard. *Reading for Academic Success: Powerful Strategies for Struggling, Average, and Advanced Readers 7–12*. Thousand Oaks, CA: Corwin Press, 2002.

Tolisano, Silvia. *Blogpost: Evolution of New Notetaking Forms*, August 12, 2015 (retrieved from http://langwitches.org/blog/2015/08/12/evolution-of-note-taking-new-forms).

Valenza, Joyce. Truth, truthiness, triangulation: A news literacy tool kit for the "post-truth" era. *School Library Journal Online*, November 26, 2016 (retrieved from http://blogs.slj.com/neverendingsearch/2016/11/26/truth-truthiness-triangulation-and-the-librarian-way-a-news-literacy-toolkit-for-a-post-truth-world/).

Worsham, Sandra. *Essential Ingredients: Recipes for Teaching Writing*. Alexandria, VA: ASCD, 2001.

Yamada, Sochichi. A study of questioning. Clark University. *The Pedagogical Seminary*, Volume 20: 2, June, 2013.

Zimmermann, Susan and Oliver Keene, Ellin. *Mosaic of Thought: The Power of Comprehension Strategy Instruction*. Portsmouth, NH: Heinemann, 2007.

Taylor & Francis eBooks

Helping you to choose the right eBooks for your Library

Add Routledge titles to your library's digital collection today. Taylor and Francis ebooks contains over 50,000 titles in the Humanities, Social Sciences, Behavioural Sciences, Built Environment and Law.

Choose from a range of subject packages or create your own!

Benefits for you

» Free MARC records
» COUNTER-compliant usage statistics
» Flexible purchase and pricing options
» All titles DRM-free.

Benefits for your user

» Off-site, anytime access via Athens or referring URL
» Print or copy pages or chapters
» Full content search
» Bookmark, highlight and annotate text
» Access to thousands of pages of quality research at the click of a button.

REQUEST YOUR **FREE** INSTITUTIONAL TRIAL TODAY

Free Trials Available
We offer free trials to qualifying academic, corporate and government customers.

eCollections – Choose from over 30 subject eCollections, including:

Archaeology	Language Learning
Architecture	Law
Asian Studies	Literature
Business & Management	Media & Communication
Classical Studies	Middle East Studies
Construction	Music
Creative & Media Arts	Philosophy
Criminology & Criminal Justice	Planning
Economics	Politics
Education	Psychology & Mental Health
Energy	Religion
Engineering	Security
English Language & Linguistics	Social Work
Environment & Sustainability	Sociology
Geography	Sport
Health Studies	Theatre & Performance
History	Tourism, Hospitality & Events

For more information, pricing enquiries or to order a free trial, please contact your local sales team:
www.tandfebooks.com/page/sales

Routledge
Taylor & Francis Group

The home of
Routledge books

www.tandfebooks.com